POWER CARVING
MANUAL

The Best of **WOODCARVING**
ILLUSTRATED

POWER CARVING
MANUAL

Tools, Techniques, and
16 All-Time Favorite Projects

With contributions by Frank Russell,
Jack Kochan, David Sabol, Lori Corbett,
Chuck Solomon, and Dave Hamilton

**Reciprocating tools recreate
the look of a handcarved
project. See page 22.**

FOX CHAPEL
PUBLISHING

© 2009 by Fox Chapel Publishing Company, Inc.

Power Carving Manual: Tools, Techniques, and 16 All-time Favorite Projects is an original work, first published in 2009 by Fox Chapel Publishing Company, Inc. The patterns contained herein are copyrighted by the authors. Readers may make copies of these patterns for personal use. The patterns themselves, however, are not to be duplicated for resale or distribution under any circumstances. Any such copying is a violation of copyright law.

ISBN 978-1-56523-450-5

Library of Congress Cataloging-in-Publication Data

Power carving manual : tools, techniques, and 16 all-time favorite projects.

   p. cm. -- (The best of Woodcarving illustrated.)

Includes index.

ISBN: 978-1-56523-450-5

1. Wood-carving. 2. Power tools. I. Woodcarving illustrated.

TT199.7.P675 2009
736'.4--dc22

2009028102

To learn more about the other great books from Fox Chapel Publishing, or to find a retailer near you, call toll-free 800-457-9112 or visit us at *www.FoxChapelPublishing.com*.

Note to Authors: We are always looking for talented authors to write new books in our area of woodworking, design, and related crafts. Please send a brief letter describing your idea to Acquisition Editor, 1970 Broad Street, East Petersburg, PA 17520.

Printed in China
First printing: September 2009

Table of Contents

What You Can Make

Fantasy Projects:

Woods wizard cypress knee (page 70),

Walking stick wizard (page 110),

Whimsical house (page 131)

Holiday Project:

Santa caricature (page 60)

Birds:

Contemporary primitive loon decoy (page 66),

Killdeer (page 90), American woodcock (page 120),

Cardinal (page 136)

Jewelry:
Maple leaf earrings (page 79),
Maple leaf pin (page 113)

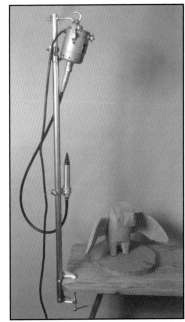

Shop Project:
Collapsible telescoping rod (page 86)

Wildlife Projects: Twig (page 97),
Dogwood leaf (page 101), Mushroom (page 106),
Black bear (page 140), Realistic habitats (page 144)

Introduction

Woodcarving Illustrated magazine presents this collection of power carving articles and resources. Whether you're just getting started in power carving or have been using power carving tools for years, the following pages offer resources and projects you'll want to turn to again and again.

This book is divided into three sections. The first section goes over the basics of safety, tools, accessories, and anything else you'll need to set up a work area and get started. If you're just beginning in power carving, you'll want to start with the first section. The second section is a set of articles focused on techniques, from basics cuts to texturing feathers. The last section offers projects to try out your newly learned techniques, hone your existing skills, or simply find inspiration for your next carving project.

Carving a Dogwood Leaf, by
Kenny Vermillion, page 101.

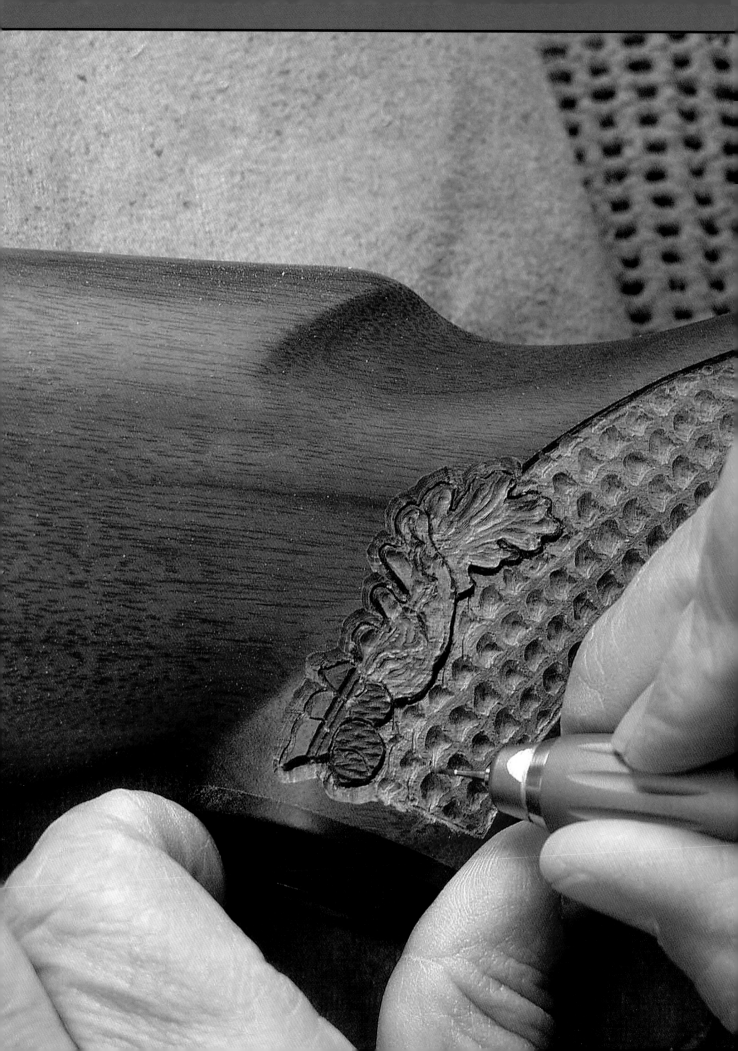

Getting Started in Power Carving

Carving with power involves the use of motorized equipment that rotates a shaft with a cutting bur mounted on the end. Because the rotating bur grinds away wood in a very controlled manner, power carving allows you to create delicate designs and intricate details that would be extremely difficult to carve with traditional tools.

Contributors to this chapter include: Dave Hamilton, Jack Kochan, Frank Russell, Roger Schroeder, and Chuck Solomon.

Air turbine units provide precision control. See page 20.

The use of power tools became more common among carvers in the 1970s. About 90% of bird carvers use power for some or all of their carving. Carvers who specialize in mammals, fish, humans, and interpretative carvings also use power for carving.

In addition to affording you more control, power carving tools generally remove wood faster than traditional edge tools. They also let you create thin carvings and achieve highly detailed pieces. It is possible to accomplish similar effects using edge tools, but it is much more difficult. Power tools carve in areas, such as tight recesses, where it is nearly impossible to fit traditional tools. For example, it's much easier to create a delicate hummingbird bill without breaking it, when using power; however, one small slip with a knife or gouge and the bird's bill is destroyed. Power carving does not preclude the use of edge tools, but enhances your ability to achieve desired effects in your carving.

In addition to the effects possible with power carving tools, carving with power opens up a world of opportunities for carvers with arthritis

Power carvers can create thin delicate carvings. This hibiscus was carved by Wanda Marsh.

Power Carving Pros and Cons

Power carving offers several advantages over carving with hand tools, but there are drawbacks. It's important to weigh all of the factors involved and make an informed decision. When possible, experiment with the tools and techniques before investing in power carving equipment.

DRAWBACKS OF POWER CARVING
- Involves a higher initial investment
- Has specific safety concerns
- Creates noise
- Generates dust

BENEFITS OF POWER CARVING
- Removes wood quickly and with precision, especially when using hardwoods
- Minimizes splintering and fracturing of the wood
- Provides greater control than knives or gouges when carving fine detail
- Allows carving and grinding of metal and epoxies
- Provides quick and controlled sanding
- Eliminates the need for sharpening
- Provides an alternative for carvers who have difficulty with edge tools due to arthritis, etc.

or limited hand strength. You must be committed to taking the proper precautions when it comes to safety, but power carving offers rich rewards and can greatly enhance your enjoyment of carving wood.

Power carving can also be a boon to those who hate to sharpen. With power carving, you can easily carve the hardest woods without ever stopping to sharpen your tools.

If you've been thinking about using power tools for the first time or expanding your collection of power tools, this section can help you get started. Included here is what you'll need to know to set up a safe work environment, find the right tools, and select the right bits and accessories.

Safety

Safety is the first consideration of this book, and it should be for any shop or working area. All types of carving involve some risks. Being informed and taking the proper precautions will keep you safe and enhance your carving experience.

Most woodcarvers have at least a table saw or a radial arm saw to cut carving stock into manageable pieces, and a band saw for blanking out. Many also have a jointer and/or planer in addition to a drill press to smooth out and assist with different aspects of joinery. Every one of the machines mentioned has the capability of inflicting permanent and debilitating injuries, and care must be given to each machine in its turn with respect to safety through use, location, surrounding area, accessory use/storage, safety devices, electrical setup, blade guards/guides, and waste disposal.

It is not the scope of this book to consider safety aspects of large machinery, but I would feel remiss by not mentioning these areas of danger found in the shop or work area. Safety can never be overemphasized.

The primary safety considerations for power carving are the quiet but deadly ones: dust inhalation and fire hazard resulting from improper dust collection and disposal. We'll also discuss what safety items you should wear while carving.

Dust

The inhalation of dust is the biggest risk power carvers face. Cutting, grinding, and sanding all generate dust. The small particles of wood that remain in the air can cause respiratory problems when inhaled.

Asthma, allergic reactions, and long-term risks, such as lung and throat cancer, are all associated with dust inhalation. While the more serious risks are normally associated with exotic hardwoods, you should always take dust control seriously.

It is imperative that you use a good dust collection system. These systems operate like a vacuum, pulling air and dust particles into the system and trapping the particles in a filter. Dust collection systems come in all sizes and price ranges. Some are portable and can be moved easily. Others are larger and are incorporated into a complete workstation. There are also some large dust control machines that can be installed in the ceiling and operated remotely.

No dust control system will trap all of the dust particles generated while carving, so power carvers should wear a dust mask in addition to using a dust collection system. Whatever mask you choose, be sure it creates a good fit or seal between your face and the mask, has an exhaust valve, is made of face-friendly material, and has adjustable straps. Choose a comfortable mask and wear it when carving.

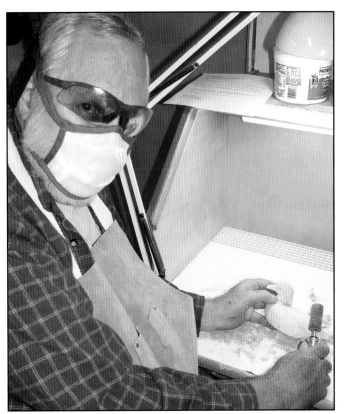

Safety equipment, such as a leather apron, dust mask, and safety glasses, should be used with a dust collection system.

Fire Hazard

Fire hazard is a danger related to dust, because it occurs where dust is not collected and disposed of. Uncontrolled and uncollected, airborne dust particles settle and build up on any exposed area or item. In a studio workshop, where all aspects of carving are dealt with, many situations can generate a spark.

A few worthy of consideration are:

- electrical motors and any heat- or spark-generating electrical appliances
- switches, outlets, and lightbulbs
- sparks generated from grinding metal when sharpening tools
- assembling metal armatures, bird legs, and supports with a soldering iron or torch
- heating elements
- torches used for soldering and bit cleaning
- improperly stored finishes
- spontaneous combustion from improperly discarded or uncared for finish rags, brushes, and wipes
- a tobacco smoker

Where smokers are concerned, "Don't worry, I'll be careful," isn't enough when a good portion of my livelihood can be affected by someone else's accident or carelessness. I have several highly visible "Absolutely No Smoking" signs prominently placed in my studios, and they have never been challenged.

Anywhere dust has settled, a fire path exists from the spark or flame source to anything combustible within the shop, and finally to the building itself. The answer to this type of hazard, of course, is to treat dust immediately as it is generated, direct it to a location for disposal, and not allow it to settle anywhere but where we want it. Even then, the shop should be inspected and cleaned whenever casual dust is observed, and dust from partially uncollected or uncollectible sources, like a table saw, should be cleaned.

Face and Eye Protection

When using any power equipment, always wear safety glasses to protect your eyes from flying debris. It is particularly important for power carving because the rotation of the bur is usually toward your face and therefore will propel particles in that same direction. Safety glasses or goggles, especially ones with side shields, will protect your eyes from dust and wood particles as well as particles of metal or material from the burs. Very rarely, the bur fractures during carving and pieces of material are thrown into the surrounding environment. Some carvers prefer real glass to plastic lenses because they find that glass doesn't have as much static electricity that holds wood dust to the lens the way plastic does. Some also prefer to wear a full face shield for some or all of their carving.

Body Protection

The greatest potential for injury occurs when large carbide or steel burs are used to remove wood quickly. The tool can slip or jump, especially when cutting into end grain. Carving with the grain is the safest way to use power and to minimize the potential for accidents. Clamping your project down when using large aggressive bits is also a good idea.

A leather apron protects power carvers and their clothes from cuts and tears. Avoid loose fitting clothes and tie back long hair. The use of a carving glove is not recommended because it can be dangerous if the fibers get caught in the equipment. Most newer micro motor carving equipment contains breakers or fuses that will stop the machine from rotating in such cases.

Creating power-carved sculptures like this one can produce flying debris, which the power carver must always be protected against.

A Guide to Power Carving Tools

You need a basic understanding of the tools before you can begin carving with power. The majority of power carvers use flexible shaft machines and micro motors. Both of these tools use a rotating bit or bur to remove wood. Flexible shaft machines have greater torque, but less speed, than micro motors. Specialized tools, such as angle grinders and air turbine machines, are also available for artists seeking specific results.

Flexible shaft machines have the power necessary for roughing out carvings as well as doing detail work. A flexible shaft machine is usually the first piece of equipment purchased by new carvers. The micro motor is primarily used as a detailer, although with a little patience it can be used to do rough shaping on small carvings. Many carvers invest in a micro motor as they gain experience. The higher speed of the micro motor produces cleaner cuts when carving fine detail.

It's impossible to say one model is better than another because it depends on what you want from your equipment. Think of it as buying a new car. Many people have brand preferences and each individual weighs features differently. Some people value gas mileage and efficiency, while others are looking for performance and durability.

Some tools make it easy to get started in power carving because of low initial cost. Other tools allow you more flexibility with a variety of available accessories. This article provides an overview of the equipment available and focuses on the models recommended for beginning carvers.

Flexible Shaft Machines

The flexible shaft machine is the mainstay for power carving. Many power carvers use a flexible shaft machine for all of their power carving needs. We recommend you invest in a flexible shaft machine unless you plan to carve mainly small or miniature carvings. For small carvings less than 3" in height, a micro motor may fulfill your equipment needs.

The flexible shaft machine consists of an enclosed drive motor attached to a 36" or longer flexible shaft. A handpiece is attached to the shaft, which is covered by a polyethylene or neoprene sheath. Benchtop units are available, but the motor unit is about the size of a softball. Most carvers opt for the hanging units to free up space on their workbench. The rotational speed of the bur is controlled by a foot pedal or a dial.

The speed at which the shaft turns the bur is measured in revolutions per minute (rpm). The higher the rpm, the faster the bur will remove wood. Torque is the power behind the rpm. Flexible shaft machines range in power from

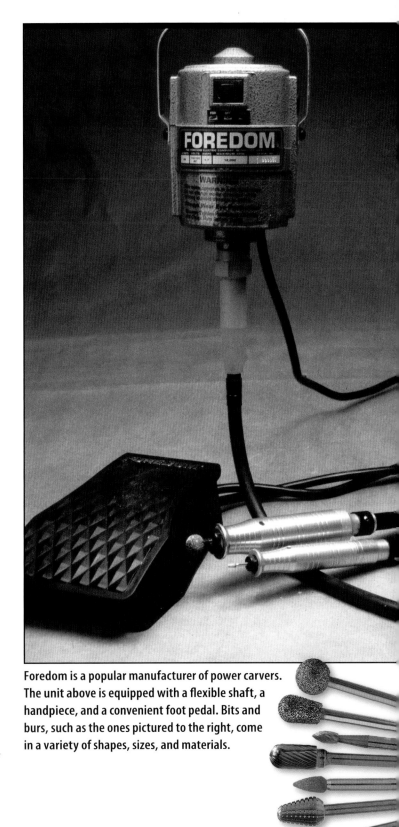

Foredom is a popular manufacturer of power carvers. The unit above is equipped with a flexible shaft, a handpiece, and a convenient foot pedal. Bits and burs, such as the ones pictured to the right, come in a variety of shapes, sizes, and materials.

Flexible Shaft Machine Handpieces

Handpieces come in a variety of sizes and shapes. Many manufacturer's handpieces are interchangeable with different brands of flexible shaft machines. The handpiece is the part of the tool you hold, and it should be comfortable to grip.

The handpiece connects to the flexible shaft on one end and secures the bit or bur in a collet on the other end. The bit or bur is the part that does the actual carving.

Most, but not all, handpieces accept varying size bits by changing the collet. Burs with large diameter shanks are primarily used for roughing out. Switch to a smaller collet or handpiece to accommodate burs with smaller shanks for shaping and detailing.

Some handpieces have a quick-change lever to expedite changing burs. However, most handpieces with this option will only accept a single shank size. Several manufacturers produce handpieces that utilize a geared three-jaw chuck. Similar to the three-jaw chuck on a drill press, these handpieces can hold any size shank accessory up to $\frac{5}{32}$" diameter. This feature is quite useful for drill bits and other bits of nonstandard size.

As technology improves, handpieces are becoming more versatile. Some handpieces have an attachment that transforms them into mini-belt-sanders. Several manufacturers make a specialty handpiece that houses a reciprocating hammer-type mechanism. These handpieces accept a range of chisels used for power chisel or gouge carving. Reciprocating handpieces should only be used with the motor rotating forward.

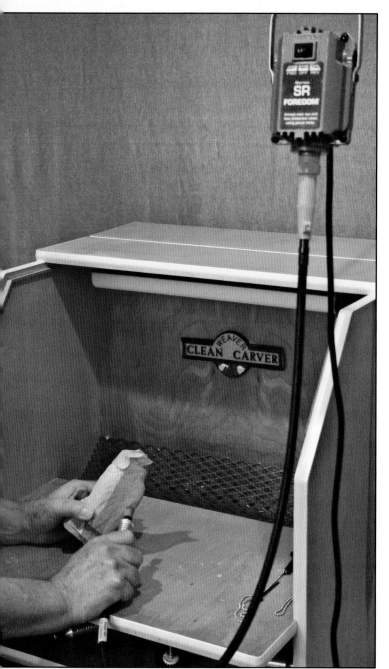

The handpiece on a flexible shaft machine is connected to the motor by a rotating shaft that is enclosed in a neoprene sheath.

$\frac{1}{15}$ horsepower to $\frac{1}{3}$ horsepower. Higher horsepower units will keep the machine from losing rpm while you are carving. If you plan to carve primarily hard wood, such as maple, choose a $\frac{1}{3}$ horsepower machine so the bur does not get bogged down in the dense wood.

Most machines have a forward and reverse setting. You want to keep the bur rotating toward you for maximum control. Reversing the direction allows you to carve with the grain when its direction changes, and it helps remove a stuck bur or drill bit. The reverse setting is also handy for directing dust away from you, toward the dust collector, while sanding.

A variety of handpieces, such as these units from Foredom, allow you to rough out your carving and add final details using the same flexible shaft machine.

At-a-Glance: Flexible Shaft Machines

Below you'll find an overview of the models we recommend for beginners from each manufacturer. Important factors to consider when shopping for a flexible shaft machine are reliability, availability of parts and service, speed, accessories, warranty, and cost.

FOREDOM 5240SR

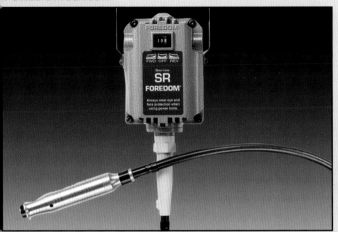

- 18,000 rpm (max.)
- ⅙ hp motor
- Wide variety of accessories available

$

Foredom also makes a ⅓ hp TX series. Both SR and TX series offer benchtop and hanging units.

MASTER CARVER BASIC

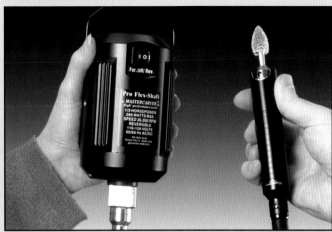

- 26,000 rpm (max.)
- ⅓ hp motor
- Moderate variety of accessories available

$

Master Carver offers Pro and Ultra units that have identical motors, but include additional handpieces.

PFINGST CH

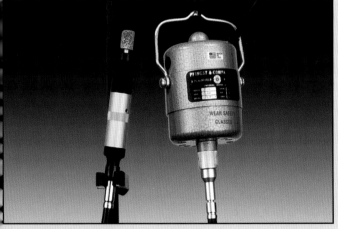

- 14,000 rpm (max.)
- ⅒ hp motor
- Limited accessories available

$

Discontinued ⅛ hp units manufactured by Pfingst may still be found at some retail locations.

WECHEER MODEL 340

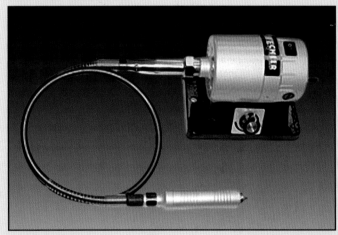

- 26,000 rpm (max.)
- ¼ hp motor
- Moderate variety of accessories available

$

$ = $200–300
$$ = $300–500
$$$ = $500–1000

At-a-Glance: Micro Motor Machines

We have listed the model from each manufacturer that we believe is best suited for beginners. Many manufacturers offer a range of models.

Major factors to consider when shopping for a micro motor machine are reliability, diameter and weight of the handpiece, rpm, service and parts availability, warranty, and cost.

BRASSELER MIO

COLWOOD RENAISSANCE WORKSTATION

FOREDOM 1070

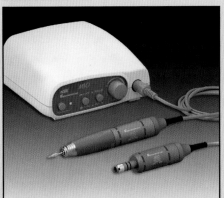

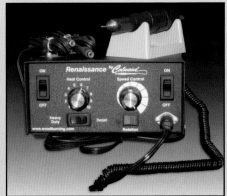

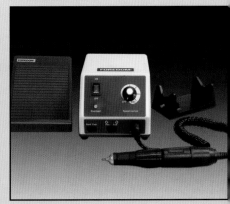

- 35,000 rpm (max.)
- Accommodates ³⁄₃₂" shank burs (optional collets include ¹⁄₁₆" & ¹⁄₈")

$ $ $

Brasseler produces four units marketed mainly to the dental industry.

- 35,000 rpm (max.)
- Accommodates ¹⁄₈" and ³⁄₃₂" shank burs (optional collets include ¹⁄₁₆" & ¹⁄₈")

$ $

This is a combination woodburner/micro motor unit.

- 38,000 rpm (max.)
- Accommodates ³⁄₃₂" shank burs (optional collets include ¹⁄₁₆" & ¹⁄₈")

$ $

Foredom provides a second model with a maximum rpm of 50,000.

Micro Motor Machines

Micro motor machines achieve speeds up to 50,000 rpm from a motor housed in the handpiece. Power is provided through a control box that includes an on/off switch, a dial or digital speed control, and a foot control/manual switch. The most expensive models have digital output. Although digital output is great for speed consistency, the cost may not justify the feature.

All of the machines outlined above include forward/reverse settings, overload protection, and a foot pedal. Some manufacturers only include one collet with their units. The additional collet may cost up to $60. Carvers seldom use a foot pedal to control the speed of the unit. Instead, most carvers set the speed manually so they can later repeat a specific speed to ensure the consistency of their carving and texturing.

Micro motor machines do not usually have high torque compared to flexible shaft machines and should not be used for roughing out large carvings. Micro motors operate at much higher speeds than flexible shaft machines. The handpiece on a micro motor may look heavier than the handpiece on a flexible shaft tool, but it is actually smaller and lighter, making micro motors easier to control. The connection between the handpiece and the power unit

on a micro motor machine is a lightweight electrical cord as opposed to the heavier connection of the flexible shaft machine. These features make it easier to use a micro motor for extended periods of time.

Micro motors are used primarily for detail carving and texturing. The majority of bird carvers use micro motor machines for the highly detailed texture characteristic of that style of carving. The higher speed of micro motors produces cleaner cuts.

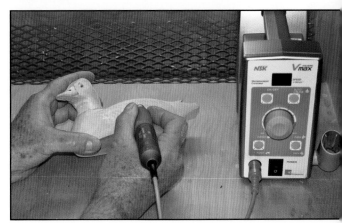

The handpiece on a micro motor machine is connected to the power supply by a lightweight electrical cord.

GESSWEIN MARATHON HANDY 700

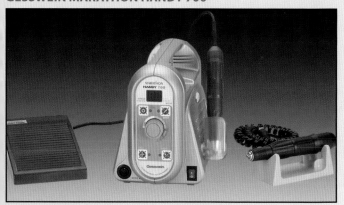

- 50,000 rpm (max.)
- Accommodates ⅛" shank burs (optional collets include ¹⁄₁₆" and ³⁄₃₂")

$ $ $

Gesswein offers three additional units ranging from 35,000 to 55,000 rpm.

MASTERCARVER MICRO-PRO

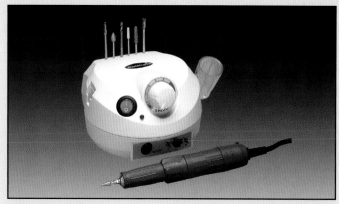

- 46,000 rpm (max.)
- Accommodates ⅛" and ³⁄₃₂" shank burs

$

Mastercarver also produces a woodburner/micro motor combination unit.

NSK V-MAX

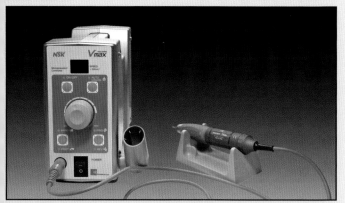

- 35,000 rpm (max.)
- Accommodates ³⁄₃₂" shank burs (optional ⅛" collet)

$ $ $

NSK produces three additional units ranging from 35,000 to 50,000 rpm.

OPTIMA 2

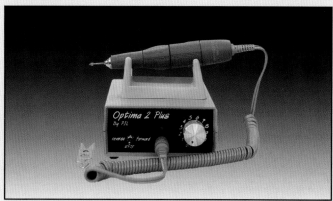

- 45,000 rpm (max.)
- Accommodates ⅛" and ³⁄₃₂" shank burs (optional ¹⁄₁₆" collet)

$

PJL Enterprises also manufactures the Ultima, a combination woodburner/micro motor unit.

RAMPOWER 45

- 45,000 rpm (max.)
- Accommodates ³⁄₃₂" shank burs (optional collets include ¹⁄₁₆", ⅛", and 3mm)

$ $

Ram Products manufactures ten different units ranging from 20,000 to 45,000 rpm.

TPS SYSTEM

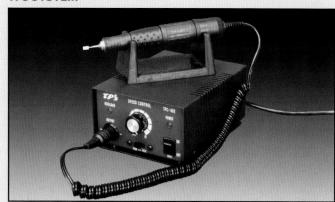

- 35,000 rpm (max.)
- Accommodates ⅛" and ³⁄₃₂" shank burs

$ $

Razertip carries a Grande micro motor kit with a maximum of 50,000 rpm.

Specialized Equipment

Flexible shaft and micro motor machines are the most common tools used by power woodcarvers. However, there are several self-contained handheld rotary tools including the models manufactured by Proxxon. There are also several types of specialized power tools employed by woodcarvers with specific needs.

Air Turbine Machines. Air turbine machines operate at up to 400,000 rpm and require the use of an air compressor. A foot pedal regulates the speed of the bur. Kits generally include a handpiece, regulator/filter, foot control pedal, hose, and lubricant. The handpiece accepts only ¹⁄₁₆"-diameter shaft burs. Only special friction grip burs rated at 350,000 to 400,000 rpm should be used in air turbine machines.

Air turbine units remove a small amount of material quickly and with great precision. Do not try to rough out a carving with an air turbine tool. In addition to wood, air turbine machines are used to carve egg shells, glass, ceramic, bone, antler, and metals. Air turbine machines are highly specialized tools and are generally purchased by carvers with specific carving needs, such as gunstocks.

Several manufacturers, such as Turbocarver, SMC, Powercrafter, and NSK, produce air turbine machines.

Carvers often use angle grinders to create detail in large chainsaw sculptures.

Air turbine units provide precision control for carving materials such as wood, egg shells, and glass.

Angle Grinders. Angle grinders are used to remove a substantial quantity of wood quickly and efficiently using a large carbide disc or toothed chain (similar to a chainsaw). Several manufacturers, including Arbortech, Friction Coatings, and King Arthur Tools, manufacture these types of discs, which can be used in nearly any angle grinder. Most tool manufacturers, including Black & Decker, DeWalt, and Bosch, make angle grinders.

Using an angle grinder requires the use of both hands to hold the grinder, so the wood being carved must be clamped securely. It is important to wear safety glasses, a dust mask, leather gloves, leather apron, and other protective clothing when using an angle grinder. Chainsaw carvers frequently use an angle grinder to detail their carvings.

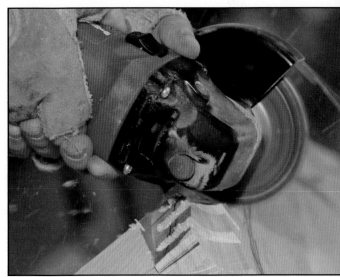

Choosing Your Power Carving Equipment

Whenever possible, test drive several different brands and models before making a purchase. Many stores and woodcarving shows provide consumers with the opportunity to try before buying. Pay attention to the comfort and weight of the handpiece. Try carving both hard and soft wood to determine the tool's ability to remove wood quickly. The equipment should not lose power even at low speed. Neither the handpiece nor the motor should vibrate or generate uncomfortable amounts of heat. Make sure the noise level is acceptable and determine how easy it is to remove and replace the handpiece and bits.

In addition to the overall quality of a tool, research the availability of technical support as well as parts and service. Does the manufacturer offer a toll-free number to call if your tool stops working? Is there a website you can visit to find tips and techniques for using and maintaining the tool? Be sure to think about what happens after the initial purchase.

Consider how much time you will be carving. Ask other carvers in your woodcarving club for their personal opinions or visit websites, such as the *Woodcarving Illustrated* forum (*www.woodcarvingillustrated/forum*), where you can gather testimonials from a large group of power carvers. Keep in mind, though, that reviews from carvers are personal opinions and can vary in reliability.

In most cases, buy the best equipment you can afford. Generally, inexpensive tools wear out sooner and have to be replaced, therefore doubling your cost. Once you have decided on the unit you want to purchase, check with retailers for discounts or special package-deal pricing. The purchase of a power carving unit is an investment. With proper research, you can find a unit that will provide years of dependable performance, allowing you to concentrate on honing your carving skills.

CHECKLIST FOR POWER CARVING EQUIPMENT

- ☑ Comfortable handpiece
- ☑ Generates little vibration and heat
- ☑ Acceptable noise level
- ☑ Adequate technical support
- ☑ Availability of parts and service

Reciprocating power carvers add hammer-like action to traditional-edged tools.

Reciprocating Carvers. Reciprocating carvers are self-contained electronic units that use interchangeable chisels or gouges to remove wood. Generally, reciprocating carving units are held with both hands, so the wood being carved must be clamped. Reciprocating carvers allow you to produce a tooled surface, similar to the one produced by traditional hand tools, without as much effort. Arbortech, Flexcut, and Automach each have stand-alone reciprocating carvers. If you have a flexible shaft machine, you can purchase a reciprocating handpiece that simulates the function of a reciprocating carver on a small scale.

Woodburners. Woodburners usually consist of a power unit, a cord that attaches to a handpiece, and a tip or tips that fit the handpiece. The handpiece is often held like a pencil and used to augment the texturing and detail made with a power carving machine before any paint is applied. Bird carvers find woodburners particularly useful in their craft for creating lifelike feathers. There are a number of woodburner manufacturers, and each unit has different features to consider depending on your specific needs.

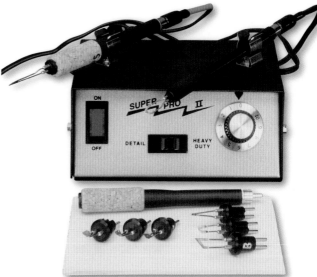

Woodburners usually consist of a power unit, a cord that attaches to a handpiece, and different types of tips. These units are often used to amplify texturing of hair, fur, and feathers.

Choosing the Right Bit

Just as there are a variety of power tools available from a variety of manufacturers, there are many bits offered in different shapes, sizes, and materials. Some materials are as hard as diamonds and some as fragile as ceramic. The bits go by names such as burs, cutters, carvers, stones, and disks. While the descriptions may seem baffling, all bits perform the same important operation: wood removal. Once you have the nomenclature mastered and acquire an understanding of bit composition, including the fact that "grit" is used here as it is when referring to sandpaper grade, the rest should be easy to follow.

To help you with making choices, first ask yourself the following questions:

- How fast do I want to remove wood?
- How much wood do I want to remove?
- How smooth do I want the finished surface to be?
- Which size and shape is best to use for a particular job?

Bit Types

One way bits are classified is by material. Different materials—carbide, ruby, diamond, steel, stone—cut with different levels of aggressiveness, have different grits within the materials, and are better at certain tasks than others.

Among the bits available are tungsten carbide burs. A distinguishing feature is points or "teeth" that are either randomly spaced or in perfect alignment. Two of the best-known brands are Kutzall and Typhoon. The Kutzall burs are offered with three colored grits: silver is coarse, gold is medium, and red is fine. Typhoon burs come in three

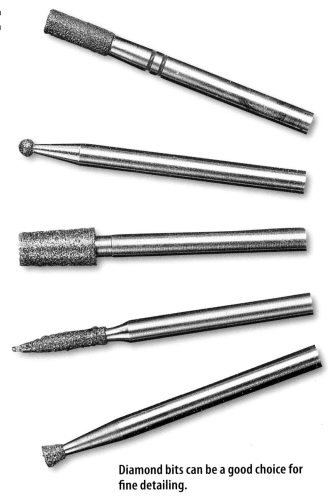

Diamond bits can be a good choice for fine detailing.

Carbide burs are aggressive cutters.

Fluted burs are designed to cut like rotary files.

Stump cutters remove wood much as fluted burs do, but more aggressively.

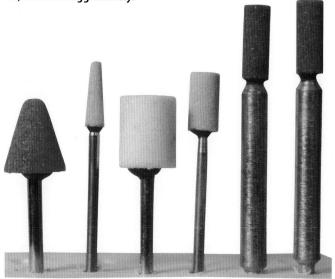

Texturing stones are made from different materials, including ceramic, and come in an assortment of textures.

grits but with some different colors: black is coarse, red is medium, and blue is fine.

A steel- or carbide-fluted bur, with rows of knife-like edges, cuts wood like a file. When the rows are parallel, the bur is described as "single cut." When rows cross each other, the bur is called "double cut." Both types are available in three grades—coarse, medium, and fine.

A variation of the fluted bur is the stump cutter, a bit that is sometimes described as a crosscut bur. Having rows of parallel, knife-like, serrated edges, the bur leaves a slightly ridged surface. Like their counterparts, these burs are also available in different grades of coarseness.

Ruby carvers and diamond bits get their names from the mineral deposits that are bonded to a steel shape and are available in various grits. Diamond bits are generally smaller in size than ruby carvers, but both types are very long lasting.

Made from silicon carbide, ceramic, or other abrasive materials, texturing stones are available in a variety of grits and are often identified by color. White stones are the finest grit and are most often used for fine detail texturing. Pink, green, and brown stones are coarser than white and are useful for fine detail shaping and smoothing. Ceramic blue stones are made from a hard material that should last a lifetime while providing a smooth finish.

If speed is your goal, tungsten carbide burs are the best choice. Unfortunately, the faster a bit cuts, the faster it gets loaded up with wood and stops cutting. Stump cutters also work well at taking away excess wood, but they are not as aggressive as their carbide cousins. However, some carvers often use fine stump cutters for detail shaping. For hogging off wood on a small scale, as well as for very fine detailing, ruby carvers and diamond bits may be a good choice.

To achieve a smooth finish, the finer the grit, the smoother the surface. For this reason, most texturing stones are ideal for smooth finishing, but finish is not dependent on bit grit alone. The other critical factor is the rotary tool's rpm. Follow this general rule: The coarser the grit, the slower the rpm; the finer the grit, the faster the rpm.

Bits, such as the ruby carvers shown here, come in many shapes.

Bit Profiles and Sizes

Bit shapes range from round to flame to needle. Choosing a shape that is best is often a matter of personal preference. A cylinder shape is excellent for smoothing a flat surface, while a round or ball-nose bit allows you to get into small spaces. Needle-shaped bits are invaluable for very tight areas and undercutting.

When it comes to choosing a size, select the largest bit that you are comfortable using. If you are hollowing a contoured area such as a spoon, for example, your obvious choice of shape is a ball-shaped bit. Using one that is only ⅛" in diameter will leave many marks on the surface that need to be sanded out. A larger bit, ½" or ¾" in diameter, is a better choice because less sanding is required.

Bit Cleaners and Cleaning Materials

Because all bits become clogged at some time or another, you'll want to keep some materials on hand for bit cleaning. A propane torch is one method used to clear clogged carbide burs.

A stiff wire or bristle brush can be used alone for steel burs or after using the propane torch for carbide burs.

Oven cleaner followed by the stiff wire or bristle brush can also be used on carbide and steel burs, and ruby and diamond bits. Simply spray the bit head with oven cleaner, let it set for twenty to thirty minutes, and then brush it.

Neoprene (crepe) rubber blocks are useful for cleaning out ruby, diamond, and stone bits. Soaking these bits in equal parts of hot water and a commercial cleaner/degreaser concentrate also works very well if the bits haven't been extremely burned in.

A mineral block (wet stone) soaked in water works well for diamond bits. Simply rotate the bit slowly on the wetted material to clean it.

A stiff bristle brush removes debris from bits.

Bit Shapes

BALL:
- Use to create concave cuts and to hollow out areas
- Creates a cut similar to a U-gouge

CYLINDER:
- Use to cut flat areas, round edges, and make stop cuts and V-cuts
- Creates a cut similar to a knife or straight chisel
- Hold the tool at an angle and use the top corner to make V-cuts
- Smooth-end or safe-end bits are the most useful

FLAME:
- Use to make concave cuts and V-cuts, and to recess areas
- Creates a cut similar to a U-gouge when using its side and a V-tool when using the tip

PEAR:
- Use to round edges and create lumps and bumps when bird carving

BULL NOSE/BALL NOSE:
- Combines a ball with a cylinder
- Use to make concave cuts and hollow out areas using the top
- Use the side to cut flat areas and round edges
- Creates a cut similar to a U-gouge with the top and a knife cut with the side

LARGE TAPER:
- Use to round edges, make concave cuts, and access hard-to-reach areas

SMALL TAPER:
- Use to access hard-to-reach and angled areas
- Create feather barbules and hair

OVAL:
- Use to round edges, create lumps and bumps, and make concave cuts

INVERTED CONE:
- Use to make V-cuts for feather barbules and hair

DISC:
- Use to undercut feathers and make channel cuts
- Cut off thin pieces of unwanted wood

Carving Accessories

In addition to the power carving tools and their bits, the items in this section can help make your carving sessions easier and more enjoyable.

Light

Give yourself and your eyes every possible benefit when it comes to lighting. Insist on quantity and quality. I try to paint in natural light whenever possible because painting is the most demanding with respect to light and accuracy of color selection, blending, and application. Whenever natural light is not available or possible, I try to come as close to it with artificial lighting as I can. A combination of incandescent and fluorescent lighting has proven to be the most effective for me over the years. I have the studio ceiling, especially in the paint area, laid out so as to provide a ratio of two 100-watt clear incandescent bulbs for every 8' double run of fluorescent lights. If, for some reason, I need additional light in the immediate area I'm working, I use swing-arm lamps to augment the ceiling lights. No matter what, I let comfort be my guide.

Shadow Light

This is a harsh light, positioned so it falls across the work and casts a sharp shadow in or across any depression or cut made in the surface of the carving. Of greatest benefit when texturing hair, fur, or feathers, shadow light gives the carver an immediate report with respect to accuracy of register, depth, and positioning of texturing cuts. Though a shadow light is beneficial to texturing accuracy and providing an additional source of light, it can strain and tire the eyes with prolonged use.

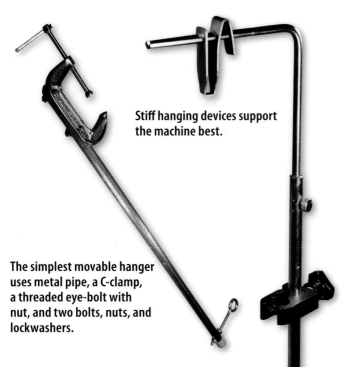

Stiff hanging devices support the machine best.

The simplest movable hanger uses metal pipe, a C-clamp, a threaded eye-bolt with nut, and two bolts, nuts, and lockwashers.

Magnifying visors help you see the fine details as you carve.

Magnification

For the fineness of detail that my carvings demand, I can no longer function with standard eyeglasses, so I have had to revert to either a light with a magnifier or my ever faithful magnifying visor.

Magnifying visors of the type shown are available in various powers, giving optimum view at different focal lengths, so select a power that will give focused magnification at a distance most comfortable to you and where you like to hold your work. I try them first wherever they are sold near me, such as hardware stores, tool vendors, or woodcarving shows. If you use them as much as I have been forced to, you want to make a proper selection to begin with.

Machine Hanger

The most common method to anchor a flexible shaft machine is to suspend it, as opposed to mounting it horizontally on a benchtop. Suspension affords far more freedom with respect to being tethered by the shaft. The hanger shown allows adjustment up or down, in or out, and at any point along the circumference of the hanger arm.

A stiff hanging device, such as the one shown, is preferred because hanging the machine on an S hook suspended on a cord or small chain will result in the machine twisting around every time it is turned on, due to the initial torque introduced when the machine is turned on.

A variety of customized homemade machine hangers can be easily made from materials found around the shop/studio, should the commercial hangers not fit your need (see page 86).

The simplest and most inexpensive movable hanger uses either metal or PVC pipe about 36" long (I use ¾" outside diameter metal conduit), a 3" C-clamp, a threaded eyebolt with nut, and two ¼" bolts, nuts, and lockwashers.

Bar clamps, telescoping aluminum channel, bent solid rod, and rigid ceiling hooks are but a few types of hangers that I have seen used.

Handpiece Holder

A handpiece holder is essential for quick and convenient placing of the handpiece while the machine is winding down after being shut off. Without a holding device that allows the carver to safely put down the handpiece, he is left holding it while waiting for the rotation to stop completely. As often as we need to stop to sketch detail on the project, change bits, or just inspect work done, a handpiece hanger or holder is a must.

Flexible shaft handpieces require a secure upright holding device, such as a pronged cradle fixture, or bench mounted clips. Equipment clips work best for securing the handpiece to the side of the bench within easy reach. I have used ½" PVC caps that were drilled and cut to size to hold the diameter of the upright handpiece, and then secured to the bench edge by flattening the back. They work beautifully (at about 24 cents each), but I have to remember to lift up, then out, and not pull straight away as with a clip.

The micro motor type handpieces require either a horizontal cradle or a tube type holder, which I prefer and consider the ultimate for giving the carver hands-off freedom. The handpiece can be placed, left in place, or removed while running without worry. The tube type holder can be made from any piece of PVC pipe that will encircle the handpiece and secure it in the position and angle desired by the carver.

A handpiece holder is quick, convenient, and safe.

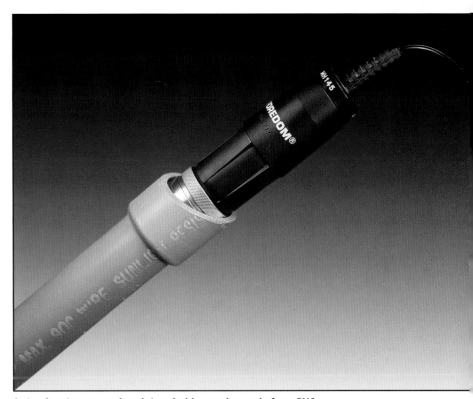

A simple micro motor handpiece holder can be made from PVC.

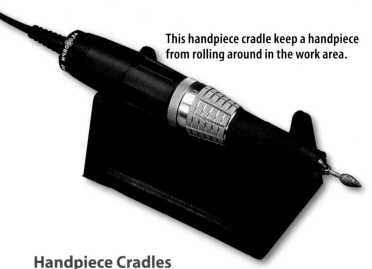

This handpiece cradle keep a handpiece from rolling around in the work area.

Bit Stand

Even with a few bits required to accomplish the different aspects of a carving, a secure organized (usually upright) bit stand is helpful so that at a glance, a needed bit can be located, easily accessed, and replaced. It is frustrating having to stop and waste time to look for a misplaced bit. I have seen bit stands made from wood, plastic, and steel, with flat, terraced, circular, sloped, and even ball-shaped presentation surfaces. Every one has served purpose and pocketbook, depending on a user preference and choice.

Handpiece Cradles

Before I begin to carve, I lay out all necessary equipment. For me, this requires setting up several handpieces, so I won't have to take time away from the project by changing bits back and forth. Until I found a way to corral those critters, at the slightest provocation, they chose to roll all over the work surface or onto the floor. So if you own one or more extra handpieces, find a convenient fixed location and mount however many cradles you need to hold extra handpieces. You will soon find you automatically reach in that direction when you want to change a handpiece. There are several ways to make horizontal handpiece cradles.

An inexpensive permanent method is to cut 6" lengths of 1½" PVC pipe in half lengthwise, sand a flat on the downward side, and screw the cradle to the benchtop with one or two countersunk screws. You can easily align as many PVC cradles as needed at very little cost.

Another inexpensive method to contain more than one idle handpiece requires a block of wood with at least 5" width and a minimum 2" thickness. The block is turned on its edge, and 1¼" holes are drilled completely through it from side to side. Drill as many holes as you have handpieces, remembering that each hole will serve two handpieces. Cut the block, still on edge, along a centerline through the holes from end to end. The result yields two grooved blocks that nicely hold and provide easy access to handpieces as they are used and replaced.

This wooden stand rotate

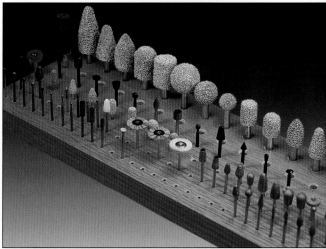

A nice bit stand can be made from wood.

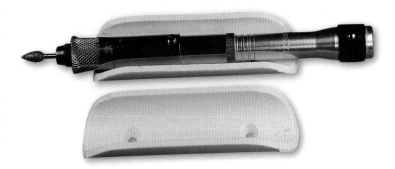

Handpiece cradles can also be easily made from PVC.

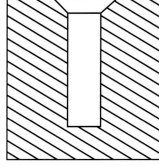

Slightly countersinking the existing hole gives an area for the bit end to fall into.

The most important aspect of any bit stand is not size, shape, or capacity, but ease of replacement and retrieval of bits. Simple straight drilled holes require more effort when replacing a bit (especially the smaller bits) among other bits, because the opening is so small. However, a hole with a "lead" for the end of the bit shank, will allow the bit end to follow into the lead and slide into the hole without any maneuvering around to find the hole. Making a hole lead requires no more than slightly countersinking the existing hole to provide an extra area for the bit end to fall into.

I prefer homemade wooden bit stands and accessory trays above all, because I can choose different woods for beautiful grain patterns, I have greater versatility with how I arrange what I want to place on the stand or tray, and I can more easily drill the bit holes to size and arrangement. If I decide to change the arrangement, wood allows me to more easily change the configuration than does metal or plastic.

To date, preference lies with a bit stand that rotates on a small Lazy Susan fixture with a square base that has sections for chuck wrenches, collets, and shaping/cleaning blocks.

Accessory Tray

Beyond machines and bits, I consider a well-organized, easily accessible, and conveniently placed (or transported) accessory tray an absolute necessity. Organized accommodation for bits and other accessories such as chuck wrenches, shaping stones, cleaning blocks, and whatever else we feel a need for, is a requirement for continuous and timesaving carving. My work surface gets cluttered enough without having to filter through several layers of debris in search of my favorite flame-shaped ruby carver.

Most accessory trays include a bit stand, handpiece cradle(s), compartments for chuck wrenches, collets, and/or corrals for shaping and cleaning block. No matter what size, shape, or layout, make sure the accessory tray serves you.

Sanding Mandrel

The homemade sanding mandrel is a neat idea I picked up from a carving seminar I was giving in Florida. I saw it in several of the student bit stands and found it was homemade and great for use on larger pieces such as duck bodies and heads. I was given one and have been using and making my own ever since.

The mandrel can be obtained from a carving vendor, or from a flea market as the ones shown here were. It has a ¼" shaft, and a ¾" rubber expanding bushing used to hold a great variety of abrasive and polishing sleeves.

The expanding consists of a fairly hard rubber bushing that fits around the shaft of the mandrel and expands as the nut is tightened upward on the reverse threaded portion of the mandrel shaft.

The homemade part of this bit consists of a foam rubber sleeve made from a short length of pipe insulation to which a size matching sleeve of sandpaper has been affixed, using double-backed carpet tape between insulation and sandpaper, and rubber contact cement as an adhesive for the sandpaper seam. Note: Make sure any overlap is lapped so that the trailing edge is away from the rotation of the machine and not into it.

The entire sanding sleeve assembly slides over the rubber mandrel bushing, and the nut is tightened just enough to firmly hold the sanding sleeve in place.

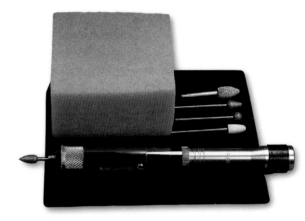

An accessory tray keeps all of your tools organized and close at hand.

A homemade sanding mandrel can be great for sanding larger pieces.

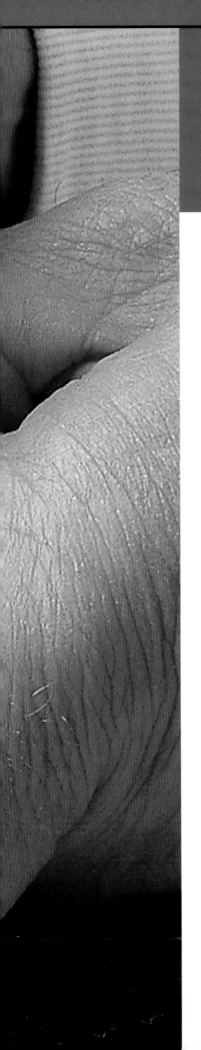

Power Carving Techniques

Whether you're just starting out in power carving or you're looking to hone your texturing skills, this section has tips from the experts to help you get the results you want.

Power Carving Bits, by Jack Kochan, page 36.

The Basics of Power Carving

By Frank Russell

Carving:

"The process of defining and refining shape by an orderly sequence of artistic cutting."

Reference Materials

Reference materials are the most important aspect to any carving—especially for a first-time subject. I constantly admonish my students to surround themselves with every photo, study skin/mount, artist's rendition, and descriptive material they can find before beginning a carving. References must be used through the entirety of the carving. "You can't carve what you don't know!"

Photo from *Realistic Dogs*, by Jack Kochan, Fox Chapel Publishing 2004.

Wasting

Wasting refers to the removal of unwanted stock. A colloquialism for wasting is "hogging," which is the removal of large amounts of wood usually in a quicker and more random manner than one would use when finish or detail carving.

Roughing

A term that refers to bringing the carving to a recognizable stage. Rough shaped denotes a general form but one without detail, texture, or refinement.

Relieving

Relieving is the act of raising a surface or shape away from a background. For example, ears are relieved from the sides of the head, and a curl is relieved from the hair mass.

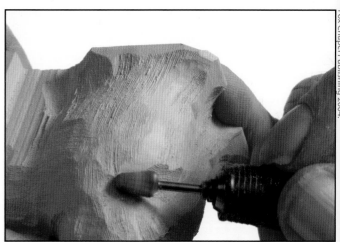

Shaping

Shaping gives refined form to a general or roughed shape. The form becomes more recognizable at this point.

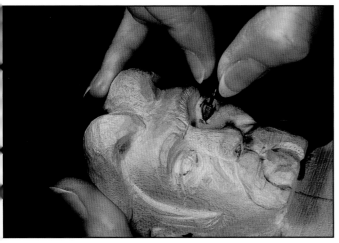

Detailing

Detailing is giving finished detail to refined shape. The detailed shape of a head, such as in the photo above, has details as required by the refined shapes—the mouth has lips, the eyes have irises and lids, the nose has nostrils, any hair mass is defined with curls, separations, etc.

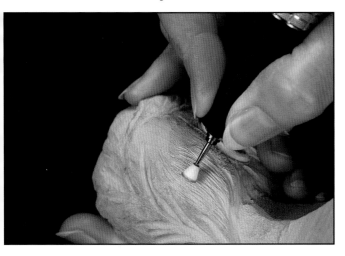

Texturing

Texturing refers to final and finishing refinement that gives character and reality to the carving. Texturing of hair, see the photo above, gives greater depth and realism to the head; wrinkles and creases on the head represent age or aging; transitional contours such as temples, cheeks, cheekbones, and chin can indicate everything from nationality to physical condition.

Using the Handpiece

For the beginning power carver, learning to control the handpiece is paramount.

Understanding the reason why a handpiece rotates in the direction it does is the first step to using it properly.

The handpiece rotation is toward the carver by necessity—giving several advantages to the user. First, the handpiece is easier to control with the rotation toward the carver, in that the power and torque of the handpiece can effortlessly be brought under sustained control. This control is usually exerted by using the thumb as an anchor point, then drawing the handpiece in the general direction of the thumb, in the same manner a knife is used (see above).

Secondly, the direction of the cut is observable because the bit cuts into the stock on the carver's side of the rotation, allowing him to view, and therefore control, depth of cut as well as amount of stock removed.

If the rotation runs away from the carver, he fights against the natural closing action of the hand by either having to open away and possibly lose control, or he has to follow the cutting stroke with his entire forearm, losing control of cut and rotation as it runs away or into the stock.

I am often asked why the reverse is necessary on a machine, and my response is that for almost all applications it isn't necessary—to a right-handed carver. For the left-handed carver, a reversible machine is a must, to my way of thinking, because it gives him/her all the advantages mentioned above that are given to the right hander with forward rotation.

Whether right- or left-handed, a habit that must be mastered and continuously used, is that of establishing an anchor or pivotal control point between the carving and the bit. Anchoring with either the thumb or little finger (depending on the cut) provides steadiness and stability to the cut that allows control.

If a wasting or shaping stroke is being executed with a large handpiece and requires a heavy "hogging" cut, the thumb must be anchored and so placed as to exercise strength and control over the cut (see **Figure 1**). If only the bit makes contact with the carving, and the whole hand is closed around the handpiece, the control and pivotal point goes clear out to the carver's elbow.

If texturing or detail shaping with the handpiece held like a pencil, the little finger must maintain contact with the carving as the pivotal or control point, or the exactness required for this type of cut is lost because the control point moves to the wrist or in some cases, to the elbow (see **Figure 2**).

There are some wasting strokes where no great amount of control is needed, and the anchor point can be lifted; except for this, precise carving can only be obtained by establishing and maintaining an anchor point (see **Figure 3**).

Optional Knives and Chisels

I always keep my hand tools within easy reach because no matter how much I love power carving—its speed, economy of effort, and its applications—there are still those few times when it is just as quick and easy to use an appropriate knife or chisel.

If I want to clean out the corner of an eye, for example, there are times when a knife will serve as well and is quicker than changing a bit. When I checker gunstocks with power, there are tight areas that the power bit will leave me to manually point up and/or finish out to an edge.

Lastly, and the biggest reason I will never be without my hand tools, is that they serve me during some wonderful times of peace and quiet. When I am in the woods or on a beach, a higher power always allows me to find a piece of driftwood or fallen branch to keep my hands busy. As I carve a face or a figure, nature works its magic around me, and my mind sorts and settles the complexities of my life.

Figure 1 - The thumb acts as an anchor point for power strokes (palm grip)...

Figure 2 - ...and the little finger acts as an anchor point for detailing and texturing (pen grip).

Figure 3 - Control is lost or reduced without an anchor point.

Be a Pro: Safety Tips

By Jack Kochan

A homemade hanger for a flexible shaft machine consists of a pipe clamp fixture, pipe and shelf bracket with a J hook end. Note that the power cord is tied back so that it does not interfere with the power carving.

On the Safe Side

Maintaining a flexible shaft machine, or any other power carving tool, is necessary to protect your investment. Still, more may be required when working with power tools. Safety is the number one issue that comes up constantly when writing or talking about woodcarving, and it cannot be ignored here. Here are some tips I employ in my shop.

Be careful of overconfidence. Many of the rotating accessories available to power carvers have the ability to remove flesh as well as wood. Most of the hand-gouging accidents I hear about are the result of feeling overly comfortable removing wood. The tendency is to push the limits of the rotary tool. Don't try to take away too much wood in too short a time or force the bit into the wood so that it slips.

Know when to clamp your project. When using large and aggressive carbide bits, such as those used to rough out, you should clamp your piece to your work bench. It is very easy to apply too much pressure with the bit, and that is when accidents happen—however, clamping will save you a lot of pain. If clamping isn't possible, then a heavy leather welding glove is recommended. Do not substitute a standard carving or Kevlar glove—just as long hair will tangle around a moving bit, so will these gloves, often causing more harm than good.

Protect yourself from wood dust. All wood dust is potentially hazardous to your health. Use a dust collector when power carving. It can be as simple as a floor fan with a pleated filter taped to the backside. If that proves to be impractical or too expensive, then a dust mask is mandatory. Paper masks are available at hardware stores and home centers, but they don't afford maximum protection.

Wear safety glasses and an apron. Safety glasses will shield your eyes from flying chips, dust, and even a small piece of a bit that can break loose. Because loose clothing often poses a hazard due to the rotating bit, don a leather apron. And if you have long hair, make sure to tie it back.

Avoid clutter. Work surfaces piled with tools and accessories distract you from knowing where that rotating bit is at all times. Knock something off your worktable or bench, and the tendency is to grab it with the hand holding the power tool's handpiece and rotating bit.

Putting Your Foot Down

A simple on/off foot switch that controls a flexible shaft machine or many other power tools in your shop is readily available and costs about $15. To operate, plug the power tool into the foot switch, which plugs into an electrical outlet. A foot switch is available for flexible shaft machines to control the rpm, making it a variable speed accessory as well. The same principle runs many sewing machines. How fast your machine operates depends on how much pressure you apply to the foot pedal.

Power Carving Hang Ups

Micro motor tools, air turbine machines, and reciprocating carvers do not need to be mounted. Thanks to the design of the flexible shaft tool, it does need to be made stationary on a benchtop or suspended from above. Solutions to mounting the flexible shaft tool include a simple hook in the ceiling; an intravenous stand; and even an overhead pipe with a mountain climber's carabiner that allows the tool to move freely across the length of the pipe. Side-mounting cradles are commercially available that hold the canister in place and keep it from rolling off the work surface. Also available are stands that clamp to the workbench and hold the canister on a hanger.

My poor man's solution to having a vertical hanger—one that cost me under $20 in materials from a home improvement center—consists of a pipe clamp fixture, a 3' length of pipe, and a shelf bracket with a J-hook at the end. The commercial models usually have a safety pin that prevents the motor canister from coming off the hanger, so a hole can be drilled into the bracket and a simple cotter pin inserted. See the Collapsible Telescoping Rod on page 86 for another option.

Power Carving Bits

By Jack Kochan

Photographs by Carl Shuman

Power carving gives a carver the speed and control to complete a carving quickly and cleanly. The following photos serve as a brief introduction to the tools, grips, and cuts used in power carving.

Flexible shaft, ball-nosed cylinder-shaped carbide cutter

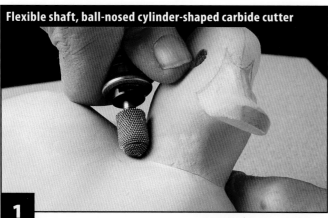

1

Rough in. Flexible shaft machines provide the necessary torque and power to complete the first step in power carving—roughing in. Here, I am using a carbide cutter on a flexible shaft machine to remove wood from the neck joint of this decoy. I am using an overhand grip, curling my fingers over the top of the tool's handle. My thumb acts as a brace against the wood, and cuts are made toward the thumb.

Flexible shaft, ball-shaped carbide cutter

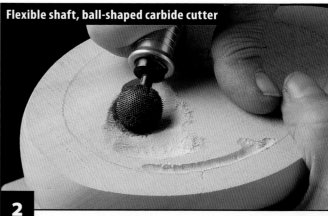

2

Remove large amounts of wood. The same overhand grip is used for any coarse work on any area of a carving. Here, I am using a large ball-shaped carbide cutter to hollow out the inside of a decoy. Cutters are often color-coded to indicate different degrees of coarseness. For this one, a Typhoon, red indicates a coarser cut than blue.

Micro motor, medium-grit cylinder-shaped carbide cutter

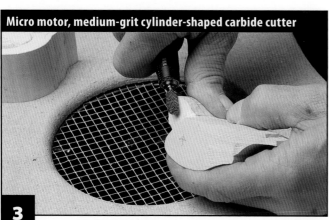

3

Do any light roughing and shaping. In this photo, I am using a micro motor, which are commonly used for light roughing in and shaping. Smaller, coarse cutters are available for smaller areas and projects. Because I am still roughing out wood, I continue to hold the tool with an overhand grip. Here, I am roughing in the head of this baby bird with a medium-grit cylinder-shaped carbide cutter.

Micro motor, medium-grit cylinder-shaped carbide cutter

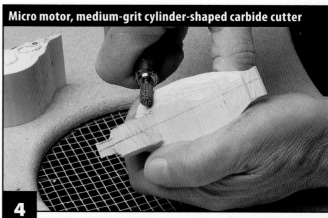

4

Continue light roughing. Here, I move on to rough out the bird's shoulder. Notice in all of these pictures that my thumb is out of the direct path of the tool. Use carefully controlled, smooth strokes, and don't be tempted to remove too much wood at once. Always move the tool, not the wood.

Micro motor, tapered stump cutter

5

Smooth and shape. Both micro motors and flexible shaft machines work well for smoothing and shaping. I use the micro motor, but notice how my grip has changed. Holding the tool as I would hold a pencil gives me greater control over the smaller, more precise movements used in this stage. My little finger acts as a pivot and support point.

Micro motor, ball-shaped stump cutter

7

Make holes and indentations. Depending on how you hold your tool, many bits and burs will give you the same result. I find that hollowing out the eye of a bird or other animal is easy with a ball-shaped stump cutter. Note that this cutter does not make the actual hole for the eye, but just the indentation. This can be followed by a cylinder-shaped cutter to complete the hole.

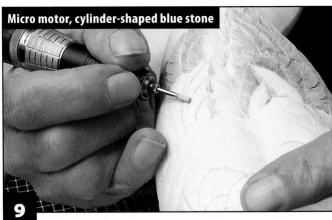

Micro motor, cylinder-shaped blue stone

9

Make flat cuts and square edges. Cylinder-shaped stones are perfect for flat cuts that require a square edge. I find them especially useful here on the wing feathers of the avocet. Each feather will have a flat, sloping surface that appears to be tucked under the previous feathers. The square edge of the cylinder adds to this appearance. This shape also works well for animal hooves and the cuffs on shirt sleeves.

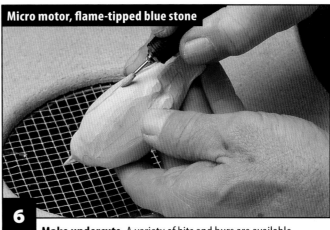

Micro motor, flame-tipped blue stone

6

Make undercuts. A variety of bits and burs are available. Matching a particular bit to the area you are working will make the tool more efficient. Here, I am using a flame-tipped blue stone to undercut the wing. I am using the side of the stone, not the very point. The flame shape of the stone allows me to cut a shallow indentation with a narrow groove.

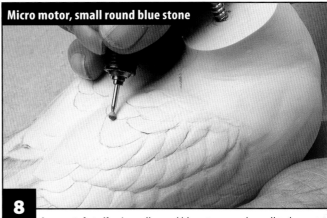

Micro motor, small round blue stone

8

Lay out details. A small round blue stone works well to lay out individual feathers. Here, I am working on an avocet. I move the stone carefully around the penciled-in edge of the feather in one smooth motion. My little finger acts as a pivot point and helps keep the tool steady. I retrace the cut to make it deeper.

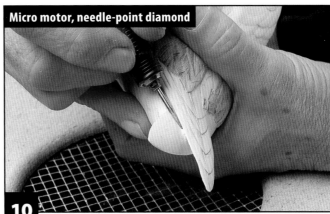

Micro motor, needle-point diamond

10

Carve deep undercuts. Occasionally, some areas of a carving need to be deeply undercut. On the avocet, I need to undercut the areas where the tail feathers overlap. A needle-point diamond works extremely well here. Note again that I am not using the very tip of the point, but the side.

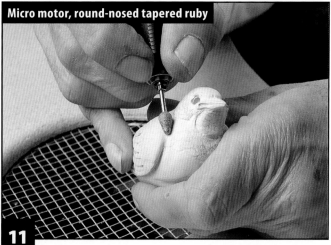

Micro motor, round-nosed tapered ruby

11 **Round a carving.** Here, I am using a ruby to round over the shoulder. Rubies are not as hard as diamonds, but depending on their grit, they can give a smoother cut. The tapered shape of this bit allows me to make a slight indentation at the shoulder.

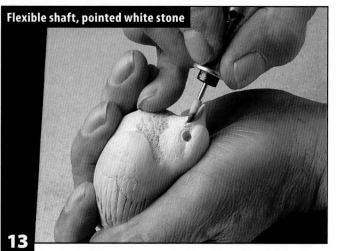

Flexible shaft, pointed white stone

13 **Continue defining.** A pointed white stone helps me define the baby bird's mouth. Again, avoid using the very point of the stone; focus on laying the tool on its side and using the surface close to the tip. Note that the tip of this stone is black. A little applied pencil lead gives an even smoother cut.

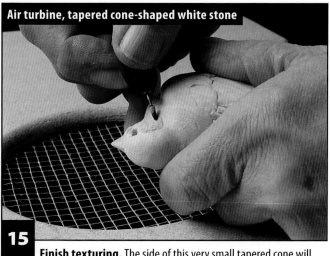

Air turbine, tapered cone-shaped white stone

15 **Finish texturing.** The side of this very small tapered cone will leave behind fine texturing marks on the cheek feathers. Pencil lead applied to the surface of the stone will give it a smoother cut.

Flexible shaft, tapered cylinder-shaped white stone

12 **Texture a carving.** Flexible shaft machines or air turbines are good choices for this next stage of power carving—texturing. Texturing requires very controlled movements, so my grip on the tool hasn't changed. I often choose softer stones over diamonds and rubies for fine detailing.

Air turbine, inverted cone-shaped white stone

14 **Detail.** An air turbine runs at much higher rpm than a micro motor or a flexible shaft and is excellent for detail work. The tan marks on the surface of this bird are the result of the friction from the high rpm. They are easily covered during painting and finishing. An inverted cone is often used to texture feathers, animal fur, or human hair.

CHANGING COLLETS **TIP**

The collet, shown here being removed from the end of a flexible shaft handpiece, can be changed to accept different-sized bits.

When the new collet is in place, the retaining collar is replaced, a bit is inserted, and the collar is tightened with the wrench. The locking pin is then removed and the tool is ready for use.

Reshaping Texturing Stones

Some carvers may find it beneficial, and even economical, to shape their own texturing stones. Jack Kochan buys cylinder-shaped texturing stones by the dozen and uses a diamond hone to create his own custom shapes.

"This way I can get shapes that are not available from the manufacturers," Jack says. "I can also avoid purchasing sets of stones. I always find several shapes in there that I never use and some that I use all the time."

Texturing stones are made from an abrasive material that is formed and molded to a cylindrical shaft. The shaft protrudes approximately one-fourth to one-third of the way into the stone. Because the material is not just embedded on the surface of the metal shaft (like ruby or diamond stones), any texturing stone can be honed to any shape—inverted cones, tapers, points, etc.

Any color stone can be reshaped as well—from the finer white stones to the coarser pink stones. To keep the "coarseness" of the original stone, Jack suggests choosing a diamond hone with the same abrasive qualities.

A cylinder-shaped white texturing stone in a flexible shaft handpiece is applied to a diamond hone to change its shape.

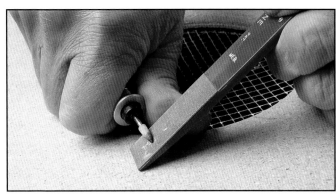

Cylinder-shaped stones can be re-shaped to tapers, points, inverted cones, and just about any custom shape needed to complete a carving project.

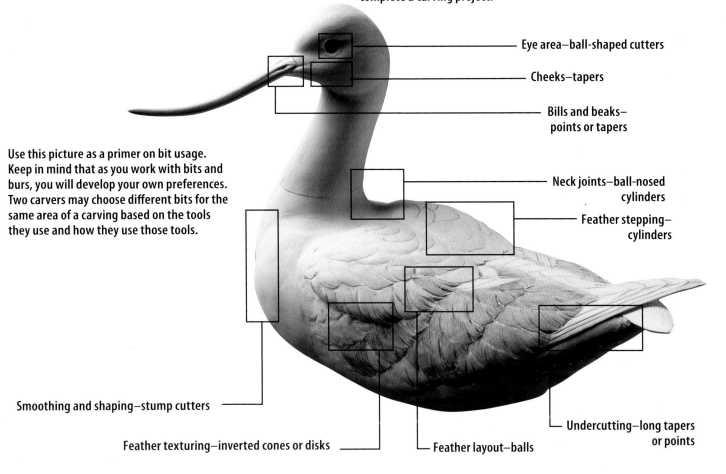

Use this picture as a primer on bit usage. Keep in mind that as you work with bits and burs, you will develop your own preferences. Two carvers may choose different bits for the same area of a carving based on the tools they use and how they use those tools.

Eye area—ball-shaped cutters

Cheeks—tapers

Bills and beaks—points or tapers

Neck joints—ball-nosed cylinders

Feather stepping—cylinders

Smoothing and shaping—stump cutters

Feather texturing—inverted cones or disks

Feather layout—balls

Undercutting—long tapers or points

Texturing Feathers

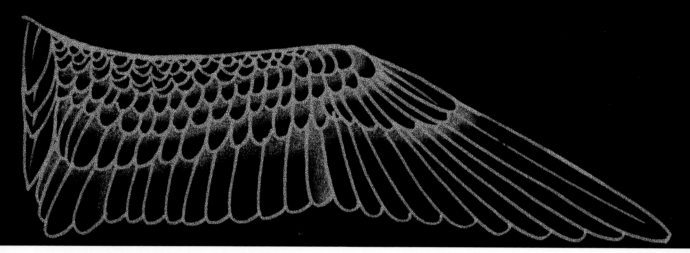

By Frank Russell

Understanding Feathers

Before you can skillfully replicate feathers on a carving, you must first understand something about them. Knowing a bit about the different types and functions of feathers found on a bird is essential to creating a realistic and accurate woodcarving. Knowing how to create feathers as a whole, in part, and as a group is a necessity to creating the pleasing effect that they produce on a carving. The higher the degree of skill you attain in this area, the greater the ease, and the greater the rewards.

Remember: You cannot carve what you don't know. Learn as much as you can about feathers as a subject. As you immerse yourself in the references required (mounts, study skins, photos, drawings) to carve a bird, you will find that this knowledge of feathers will serve you well. Ultimately, knowledge of feathers will give you a greater understanding of the bird you are carving and reduce the effort you put forth toward the completion of a fine bird carving.

Feather Facts

The main composition of a feather is keratin. Keratin is described as minuscule fibrils and larger filaments held together by an amorphous protein matrix substance. I asked a chemist friend of mine for a description of keratin in a language I could understand, and he said, it's pretty much protein . . . that's why chickens will eat feathers. Sounds like chemical talk to me.

Once a feather fully matures, its supply of blood is terminated and, similar to human hair, has no feeling.

On most birds, feathers do not cover the entire body, but are usually grouped into eight or more major groups called feather tracts. The tract areas are the tail, upper legs, leading and trailing wing edges, along the back, both sides of the underbody, and the head. The areas between these feather tracts are bare on most birds—although some birds, such as penguins, are solidly covered without these bare spaces between the tracts. Within these tracts are definable feather groups that will be described later.

There is nothing that a bird's body can do to repair broken feathers, so it must wait until a broken or old feather molts (falls off) and a new one replaces it. I have seen major flight feathers (especially primary and tail feathers) repaired by ornithologists and vets by splicing and gluing the hollow center shaft within with everything from wire to bamboo skewers.

Types of Feathers

Flight feathers are the feathers that sustain flight and maneuverability. They are the strongest feathers, and although structurally rigid, are quite flexible in length and within movement of the group. They are the main feathers found in the wings and the tail. Most of the time they are textured by woodburning owing to the desired harder, stiffer appearance that can be gained by burning as opposed to stone texturing.

Contour feathers are fan or elongated fan-shaped feathers that cover the bird's outer body. These feathers lie in such a way as to give the body a softer, rounded appearance. For this reason, many woodcarvers prefer to grind texture them with a rotary stone bit.

Down feathers lie hidden beneath contour feathers and function to insulate the bird from heat or cold. Where applicable, some advanced carvers will show just a touch of down squeezing out from beneath contour feathers in such a manner as to indicate that a feather is missing and a bit of the down has become exposed. This is done sparingly, usually no more than five or six places on an entire bird, and then only in areas known for down, such as the breast or underbelly areas.

Filoplume feathers are extremely small feathers, always hidden from view, that look like hair and are found in tufts around and at the base of certain contour feathers.

Bristle is a feather that grows almost exclusively on a bird's head and neck (see **Figure 1**). Rictal bristles grow on either side of a bird's mouth and are more pronounced on some birds than others.

Feather Functions

The feathers on a bird have four primary functions: to maintain flight, to insulate, to waterproof, and to attract. Additionally, feathers function as camouflage on some species of birds, such as the ruffed grouse, woodcock, and many female species of ducks, songbirds, and shorebirds. The camouflage is used not only to shield a nesting female, but also to guard against predators. On many species of male birds, the feather colors function in just the opposite manner, in that they are used to attract and defend. Feathers are used to attract a female during the mating and bonding period, while at the same time, their brightness is used to repel would-be suitors. Feather brilliance is also used by the male to attract and draw a predator away from the nesting site.

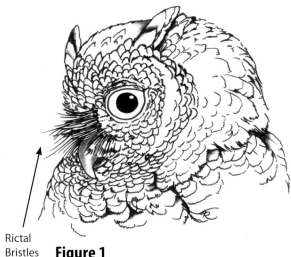

Rictal Bristles

Figure 1
Carefully observe these feathers as you carve your bird, and decide not only how prominent they are, but also, on some, how you will accomplish putting them on. Most of the time they are relieved with a fine bit, then accentuated with a woodburner (on hawks, owls, eagles). On some songbirds, it is sufficient just to paint them on with a very fine pointed brush.

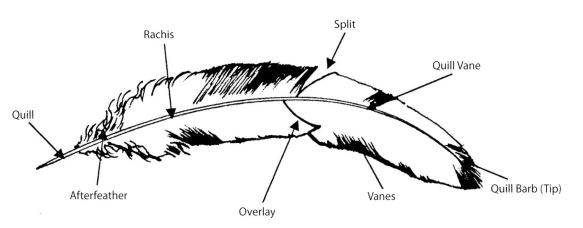

Figure 2 - Feather Nomenclature

Feather Structure

It is important to know that the outside shape of any bird's body is greatly changed by the feathers that lie within specified groups. The shape of each group (in most cases) must be determined before individual feathers can be laid out, detailed, and textured. Familiarize yourself with the most prominent wing and body feather groups and how they are shaped and flow on a particular bird.

The main stem of the feather is called the quill at its tip, rachis or shaft, vane, and barb beginning at the tip that attaches to the skin at the feather follicle. It progresses to the tip that the stiff barb end of the quill runs through (see **Figure 2** and **Figure 3**).

Running out from this main stem are parallel interlocked rays or barbs, and along each barb are even rows of interlocked, smaller raylike barbules, on which are rows of minuscule hooks or barbecels; these interlock to hold the barbs together in a network all the way around the quill. When you see a bird preening, it is realigning and interlocking all of the parts of the feather network. This network gives the feather shape and strength, and when stacked or layered against other feathers, provides enough strength to sustain the weight of the bird in flight. To gain a better understanding of this structure, fan the tail of a bird and note how the quill of each feather is positioned so as to add strength to the tail as a whole. First, you will note the tail of any bird is divided into two even sections, and each

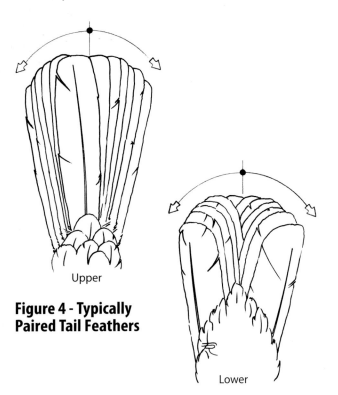

Upper

Lower

Figure 4 - Typically Paired Tail Feathers

Figure 3 - Magnified Feather Detail

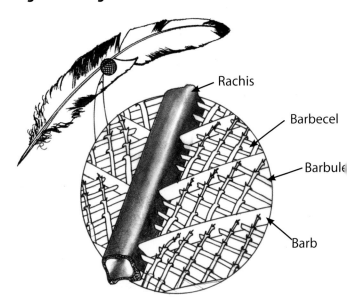

Rachis

Barbecel

Barbule

Barb

feather in one section will have a mate or counterpart in the opposite section. The result? Every bird's tail has an even number of feathers, with the vast majority having 12 for a feather count (see **Figure 4**). Most hummingbirds, swifts, and cuckoos have ten tail feathers, while a ring-necked pheasant has 18, and a grouse has 16. These feathers are also molted in pairs, so you may be hard pressed to find a bird with an odd number of tail feathers.

Before you carve a bird with spread tail feathers, you want to check the exact count necessary for the bird you are carving. These tail feathers are called rectrices. You will note that the quills are more to the center of the central tail feathers, and move more to the outside of the outer tail feathers where structurally they add greater strength to the tail for support and maneuverability during flight. These feathers not only provide lift in flight and behave as an air brake on landing, but also act together as a rudder to help steer the bird left or right. The primary wing feathers (ten on each wing) are stacked and structured in much the same way, and when viewed from this perspective, it becomes very clear how and why the feathers we consider so fragile can sustain migratory birds for thousands of miles of flight.

Figure 5 - Feathers Carved With Sharp Squared Edges

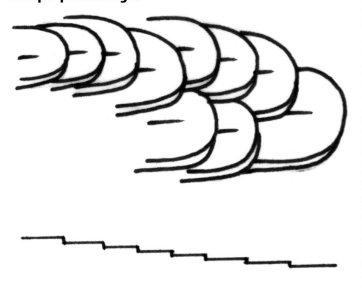

Figure 6 - Feathers Carved With Realistic Rolled Edges

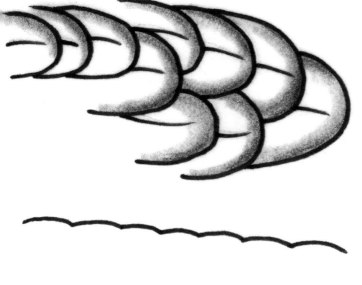

A word of caution about the possession of reference birds such as songbirds, birds of prey, shorebirds, and migratory birds, whether mounted, as study skins or frozen. A state and federal permit is required. Fines can be very severe for offenders. Check with your state's Fish and Wildlife Department, as well as your nearest Federal Fish and Wildlife Office. Gain a complete and legal understanding of what is necessary to acquire permits to obtain and possess birds, bird skins, or even feathers, before you decide to build a collection of dead birds as references to support your art form.

Sources for Study Birds

Other sources to consider for study references are museums, colleges, universities, bird societies, and nature complexes that have study collections and educational permits and are willing to share. Many have lending programs where you can borrow the skin of a bird to study both for carving and painting. The university I use allows me to borrow three skins at a time. I check them out just like books from a library, and when I bring them back (in good condition!), I can borrow others. As a rule, the university prefers not to loan mounted birds because of the fragility and ease of damage during transportation.

Feather Shape

One thing woodcarvers often lose sight of is the cupped and bent shape of feathers (see **Figure 5** and **Figure 6**). The feather, as a rule, is a rounded mound on the exposed or upper side, and cupped on the hidden or lower side, especially the body or contour feathers. The working feathers such as the primaries, secondaries, tertials, scapulars, and tail feathers also have a cupped shaped when viewed from the end, although some may flare upward away from the cup on their edges where they rest against feathers beneath them. Woodcarvers seem to drift toward the sharp, square-edged position that house shingles represent instead of creating the mounded rolling look of real feathers.

Figure 7A - Typical Upper Wing Feather Groups

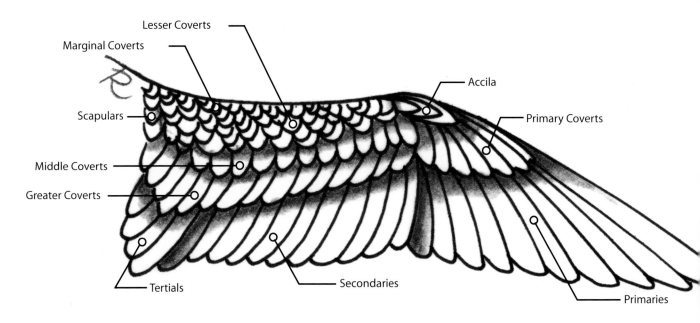

Lesser Coverts

Marginal Coverts

Accila

Scapulars

Primary Coverts

Middle Coverts

Greater Coverts

Tertials

Secondaries

Primaries

Figure 7B - Typical Underwing Feather Groups

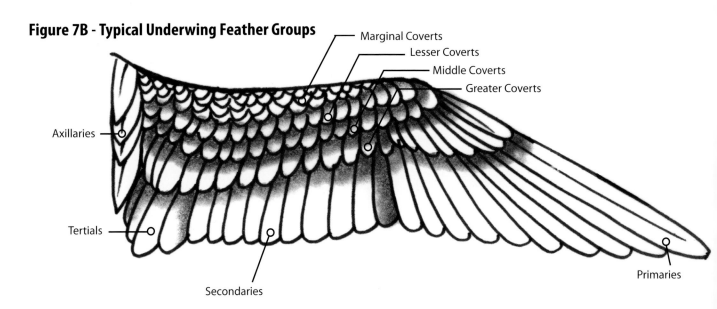

Marginal Coverts

Lesser Coverts

Middle Coverts

Greater Coverts

Axillaries

Tertials

Secondaries

Primaries

While you are viewing the harder, sharper flight feather groups, note the contours and shapes of the softer cover feather groups. Further note the contours formed within these groups by feathers that align in little groups of three or four, and others that separate themselves from the aligned ones. The "bumps" and "rolls" are endless. You will very quickly begin to formulate a method and technique as to how you want to lay out, carve, detail, and texture these same groups (and individual feathers) on your carving. When you get an idea as to how certain feathers lie, draw

them! I hear a lot of grumbling from some of my students during bird carving seminars when I have them take the time to draw on paper certain feather concepts that seem to be giving them problems during feather layout on a carving. After much shifting, erasing, and snorting, they finally draw feathers and feather placement to their (and my) satisfaction. As an instructor, I enjoy seeing the transition from frustration to relaxed enjoyment as they gradually grasp the concept of feather layout.

Feather Groups

Primaries are big, strong, heavy-shafted feathers that contribute the most to flight (see **Figure 7A** and **Figure 7B**). Usually ten in number per wing, they are most conspicuous when extended in flight; however, they are still very visible when the wing is folded. The exposed portion of the primary group very much affects the contour of the bird's back—more so on birds with longer pointed wings, such as hawks or swifts, than on birds with rounded wingtips, such as a grouse or cardinals.

Secondaries are a continuation of the primary group, along the trailing edge of the wing. Like the wings of an airplane, they provide lift and stabilize the bird's flight.

Tertials are the group of innermost secondaries closest to the body. They are usually of different shape, longer, and often a different color.

Wing coverts are feathers on both the topside and underside of the wings. On the topside, the primary coverts overlap the primaries, and the greater coverts overlap the secondaries. The primary and greater coverts are in turn overlapped by the middle coverts, that in turn are overlapped by the lesser coverts which cover to and around the leading edge of the wing. On the underside are rows of longish feathers, called the wing lining, that overlap both primaries and secondaries. The wing lining is overlapped by lesser coverts that extend and blend into the wing's leading edge and into the lesser coverts from topside.

Alula (AL-you-la) corresponds to the thumb at the joint farthest out on the front of a bird's wing. It acts as a wind slot, like trim tabs and ailerons on an airplane. The feathers are called quills and may vary from two to seven or more on some species. (The average number for waterfowl and birds of prey is three.)

Axillars, also called axillaries, are the innermost feathers on the underside of the wing next to the body. They are usually elongated in shape and are located over what would be the armpit. They fill the space between the body and the wings when the wings are spread, and can't be seen when the wing is folded.

Scapulars are usually elongated feathers that arise from the bird's shoulders on either side of the back and adjacent to each wing where they overlap the tertials and wing coverts. They help cover the folded wings, and assist in streamlining the body/wing juncture during flight. They may be of a different color or demarcation, as are the surrounding feathers.

Forehead is the area immediately above the top of the bill and the crown (see **Figure 8** and **Figure 9**).

Crown is the area on top of the head between the forehead and the occiput.

Figure 8 - Typical Songbird Feather Groups

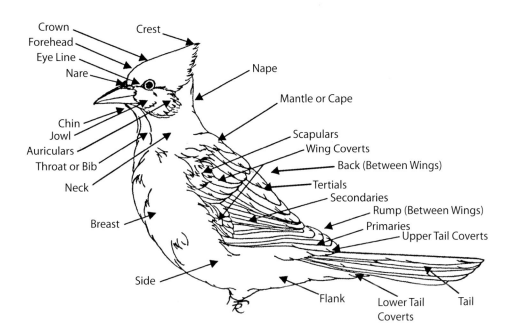

Occiput (OK-sih-put) is the back part of the head or skull.

Nape is the back part of the neck below the head.

Eye line or valley is a very pronounced indentation where the crown and forehead above meet the jowl and auriculars below to form a valley in which the eye is located. This is an important part of the head that deserves study. Not considering this area is why many beginning carvers create misplaced eyes and/or bug-eyed birds.

Jowl includes minuscule feathers that cover the area where the upper and lower mandibles (the beak) join. It sits just ahead of the auriculars and can often be evidenced by a slight depression before the auriculars begin. There is often a distinct demarcation on many waterfowl and larger bird species.

Auriculars are loosely webbed feathers on the sides of the head that cover the ear openings. If you look closely, you will find that this group (often called the ear coverts) is prominent.

Bib or Jugulum is the lower throat and that part just above the breast.

Mantle or Cape is the plumage on the back of the bird just below the nape. Ornithologically, the mantle also includes the top wing coverts.

Taxidermy Mount Problems

Be careful if you plan to use mounted birds as reference. The taxidermist can make errors, and you may incorporate his errors into your carving. One of the first ducks I ever purchased for a reference was a taxidermy mount of a standing canvasback drake with wings mounted outside of the sidepockets! My lack of knowledge at the time caused me to purchase an inaccurate mount and carve an inaccurate bird from it. I later found that the shape of the mounted head was wrong, too. I put trust in someone else's work because I had not taken the time to learn it myself. The main lesson I learned from that effort was not to do it again.

Chest/Breast/Belly includes usually rounded, soft contour feathers that begin below the bib and extend downward and around to meet the side and flank feathers. There are at least three important things to observe within these areas: the general shape of the feather, the look of softness, and the overall size of the feathers that get progressively larger as they progress through the chest into the breast and begin to diminish as they near the flank.

Side includes large, rounded, and fanned contour feathers. They are very conspicuous for size and softness and, depending on species, are strikingly marked on some species, especially waterfowl. This group is often called the side pocket on waterfowl because as the duck lands and folds its wing, the folded wing is set inside the flap formed by these feathers. Songbird wings do not enjoy the extent of coverage and support from the side feathers that waterfowl do, so study placement before you carve your bird's wings.

Figure 9 - Typical Waterfowl Feather Groups

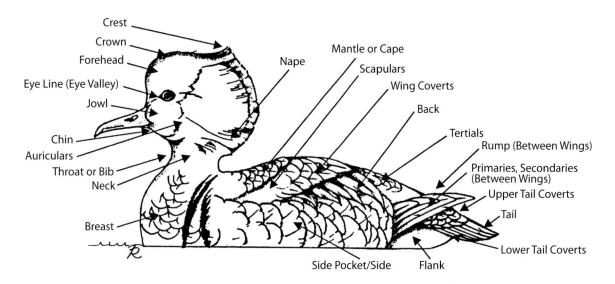

Crest
Crown
Forehead
Eye Line (Eye Valley)
Jowl
Chin
Auriculars
Throat or Bib
Neck
Breast
Nape
Mantle or Cape
Scapulars
Wing Coverts
Back
Tertials
Rump (Between Wings)
Primaries, Secondaries (Between Wings)
Upper Tail Coverts
Tail
Lower Tail Coverts
Side Pocket/Side
Flank

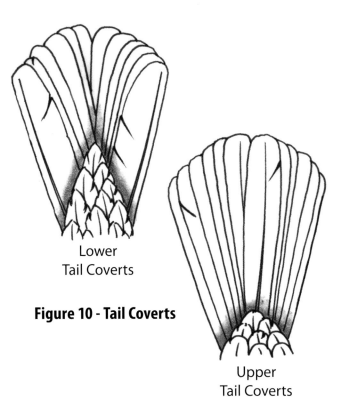

Lower
Tail Coverts

Figure 10 - Tail Coverts

Upper
Tail Coverts

Tail feathers are spread when maneuverability is needed during flight. They are not usually greatly spread when the bird is perched and at rest, unless it is preening, stretching, or displaying. However, a bit of artistic license can be taken to exemplify this feather group by spreading them enough to show the exposed area of the stems, barbs, and other feather detail such as splits and overlays.

Take the time to learn what happens to the tail when the bird is involved in the activity and pose that you wish to carve it in. The tail is extremely important to you as a carver because its position generally reflects the bird's activity. You must know what the tail does during these activities for the specific bird you are carving—activities such as normal flight, landing, at rest, displaying, preening, and defending. A good example of a special situation is mantling by birds of prey, such as a kestrel mantling over a mouse it had just caught. A bird of prey will mantle over its catch to keep it from being stolen by other predators. The body lowers into a crouch, then the wings and tail are spread down and over its catch.

Flank includes feathers that run back from the belly to become the undertail coverts, and up either side to meet the rump. If anything, these feathers are softer, yet often have a coarser appearance because of the rougher treatment they get from whatever the bird walks through, swims through, or perches on.

Rump includes the back feathers that lie below the wings and extend back to blend with the upper tail coverts.

Tail Coverts, upper and lower, cover and protect the bases of the tail feathers. Of importance to the carver is the extent to which they extend onto the upper part and lower side of the tail. Normally, the lower tail coverts extend onto the tail much farther and form a different shape than do the upper tail coverts (see **Figure 10**), a point beginning carvers often fail to notice. Also of importance is how the feathers are shaped, and how they overlap as they cover their portion of the tail.

Feather Layout

Before feathers can be drawn and finish carved, you must have some idea as to what you want the feathers to do and where you want them to go directionally. An understanding of how the feather tracts meet and meld to cover the bird's body is important before you can accurately draw and carve them.

Flow lines (see **Figure 11**) are lines drawn within the feather groups to assist the texturing process and maintain proper direction of feathers as they are laid out on a bird. It takes some study of the subject bird to establish proper direction so the feathers flow or bend not only within their group, but also overlap or join with neighboring groups to gracefully cover the whole bird.

On a duck, feather direction flows typically as shown on the sketch (see Figure 11).

Think of the bird as completely covered, but give each feather group proper direction within that covering.

In most cases, there are very distinct and noticeable division and contour lines between the major feather groups, but even though these lines exist, the feathers still maintain grace and direction. I mention grace because I believe it is important to note that some carvers are intent on showing the demarcation of the feather groups without giving enough care to how the meeting feathers interact and join to cover the bird.

Some beginning carvers are so concerned with establishing the various groups for the observer that they make the joining of the groups almost impossible with regard to how the feathers might lie on the actual bird.

Figure 11 - Typical Feather Flow Lines

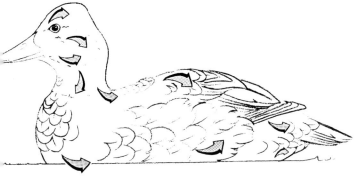

Feather Placement and Size

Many beginning carvers are told that feathers shingle one over the other; this is true, but unfortunately they lay out their feathers exactly like shingles—straight, evenly spaced, and staggered, one over the other, row after row, course after course, with little if any variation (see **Figure 12**).

Although feathers lie one over another, the vast majority are not in rows and are different sizes. Feathers, like human hairs, are always in a state of replacement and growth because some are always being shed or pulled or preened. (Now that I'm slightly older, I notice this phenomenon more and more on my comb and in my hairbrush . . . although I wait in vain for the replacement parts.)

Because of this constant change, don't be afraid to draw small feathers with and atop the larger ones within a particular feather group. This applies most particularly to the softer, nonworking feathers such as head, neck, breast, cape, flank, belly, and lower tail coverts. Typically, a group of feathers would be sketched like **Figure 13**. This mixing of feather sizes doesn't necessarily apply to the working (flight) feathers, such as primaries, secondaries, and tail. Although the change occurs, it isn't as readily noticeable because of the way the feathers are laid or stacked one atop the other. Feather ends and varying sizes of feathers are not as obvious as the smaller, softer, more visually exposed feathers.

Feather Life

Feathers must be given life in order to be attractive and flow with the group. Feathers that look stiff and straight, even though they have direction (flow), detract from a carving. I sketch a central flow line in the middle of each feather not only to create direction for layout of the entire bird, but also to keep me on track for direction of strokes while I am texturing—whether with a texturing stone or a woodburner. How well I plan these little guidelines is directly proportional to what the finished feathers do, and ultimately the final and overall appearance of the carving. For comparison, I use the previous feather layout sketch and show it with no life (see **Figure 14**), and then add life by giving each feather within the group a directional flow of its own (see **Figure 15**).

How Many Feathers?

Though it is not necessary to know an exact feather count as a woodcarver, it is interesting to note the number on some birds. More or less, a mallard duck has 12,000 feathers, while a whistler swan has 25,000. A ruby-throated hummingbird has 940 feathers, but proportionately it has more feathers per body weight than the whistler swan. Songbirds will have from 1,200 to 4,600 feathers, while the stately bald eagle, for all of its size, has fewer than 7,200. The feathers on that same eagle will have a total weight of 1¼ pounds, which is more than double the weight of the bird's entire skeleton.

Practice

Take the time to observe feathers, and then practice drawing different feather shapes, individual feathers, and groups of feathers until you are satisfied that what you have drawn represents the feathers you want to carve and texture.

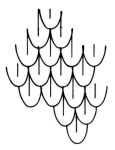

Figure 12 - Shingled Feather Layout

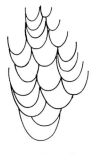

Figure 13 - Feather Layout Lines

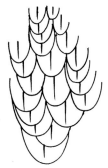

Figure 14 - Feather Layout with No Life

Figure 15 - Feather Layout with Life and Direction

Creating Hard Feathers

By Frank Russell

Burning Tips:

• If you don't feel a degree of contact with the wood, chances are you are burning too hot and will have a charred surface.

• If you feel too much friction and drag with each stroke, you are burning too cool and are not getting sufficient depth to your stroke. You will soon get tired because of the amount of pressure needed to achieve texture.

• Begin at the bottom and work upward.

• Begin at the rear and work forward.

• To maintain continuity, occasionally allow your stroke to run in the same direction as the previously textured feather below it.

Always use a light to cast a shadow across the area opposite the texturing hand. For example: If you are right-handed, position the light on your left. Every time you stroke, the light will cast a shadow on the depression, which allows you to see the progress of the texturing.

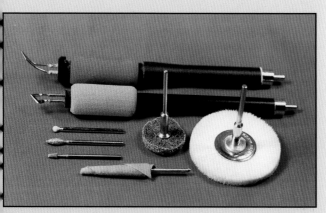

The assortment of tools I use to create hard feathers are: (top to bottom) bent skew burning tip (dull), straight skew burning tip (sharp), ball-shaped stone, flame-shaped ruby carver, tapered steel bit, 1"-diameter defuzzing pad (hard), 2"-diameter rotary brush (soft), and tapered sanding mandrel with cloth-backed sandpaper.

Hard feathers are ones that help achieve flight and maneuvering. They include primaries, secondaries, and tail feathers. Other feathers are included that sometimes embrace tertials and scapulars, depending on the species of bird and whether I want the feather to look hard.

In order to achieve a hard-looking feather, I finish texture using a burning system. The burn lines give a stiffer, more rigid appearance caused by the shallow evenness and close repetition of the burning strokes. I like a marked, but not obtrusive, differentiation between the hard feather groups and the softer-appearing feather groups found on the breast, flank, and belly.

Feature Details

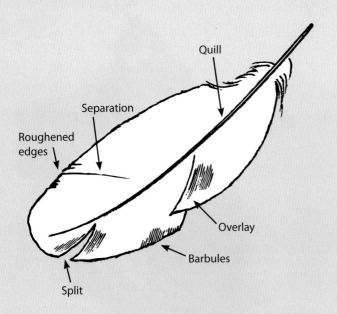

Quill

Separation

Roughened edges

Overlay

Barbules

Split

A split is a barbule separation that leaves a V-shaped opening in the feather, revealing a part of the feather below. A split is a great place to call attention to your work because not only is there a carved detail but also a place to accentuate when you paint. This is where you are able to create additional highlighting and shading on the feather.

A separation is a lesser split. A bird's natural movement causes a feather's barbules to separate. But the barbules realign without the hooklike barbecells interlocking as they do when the bird preens. The appearance is simply one of a deeper groove between the barbules. Try to establish these separations where feather groups work against or into one another.

An overlay is a separation that goes the opposite way of a conventional split. Instead of an open V shape, the upper barbules lay over the lower barbules. This creates a notch in the edge of the feather and a raised ledge where the overlay runs back to join the quill. An overlay is a nice place to draw attention to your skills. However, an overlay occurs much less frequently than a split, so don't overdo it.

Keep in mind that splits or separations can also be overdone. A few are natural, but as a rule many indicate either a sick or stressed bird. Even a storm-blown bird will preen and realign feathers before it sleeps rather than allow the feathers to go in disrepair.

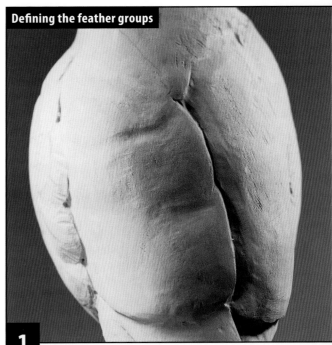

1 **Define the feather groups.** I first make sure the outer edges of a feather group appear to roll over or under the adjacent groups as they do on the real bird. I finish sand the surface to a point that allows me to easily lay out the feathers. Essentially, I give particular attention to removing all tool marks, but I maintain the shape of the overall group with a smooth and finish-sanded appearance.

2 **Lay out the feather group pattern with a pencil.** Take time to draw exactly the shape and size of feathers you want to create. If the feathers don't appear the way I want them to, I erase and redraw them. This is the foundation not only for the finished appearance of the feather group, but also for the overall appearance of the bird carving. To stress the importance of the penciled layout stage, I tell my students that one of the most important tools a woodcarver has is a pencil, and the next most important tool is the rubber eradicator on the end of that pencil.

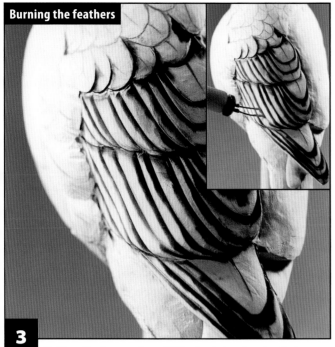

Burning the feathers

3 **Outline the lower edges.** With a bent skew burning tip (see inset), outline the lower edge of each feather within the group. I always test the intensity of the heat on a piece of scrap wood of the same species I am carving. This gives me an accurate and reliable indication of the heat setting I need.

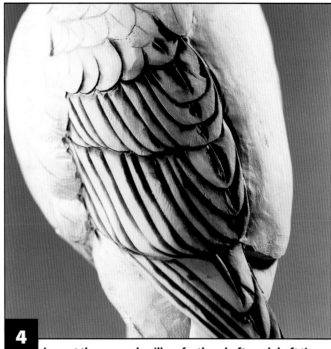

4 **Lay out the exposed quills or feather shafts and shaft tips.** Draw the bent skew tip along each side of the quill. I practice this motion on the scrap wood until I can achieve the thickness and size of the quill desired at the body end and the point that ends before the outer tip of the feather. For comfort sake, I find that drawing the burner tip toward my body creates a better feel and sense of control. I also locate and relieve feather splits, separations, and overlays now (see Feather Details on page 50).

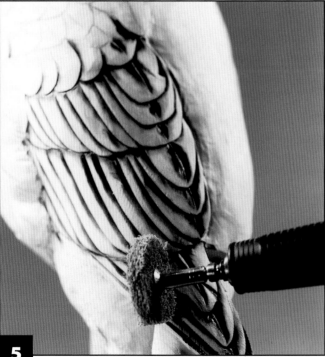

5 **Finish shape and remove any sharp feather edges.** I can achieve shaping by drawing away from the quill with the bent skew burner tip to contour the feather barbs. I break down and shape sharp edges by drawing the tip along the feather edges with a lower heat setting or I very lightly stroke the sharp edges with a defuzzing pad on a rotary mandrel.

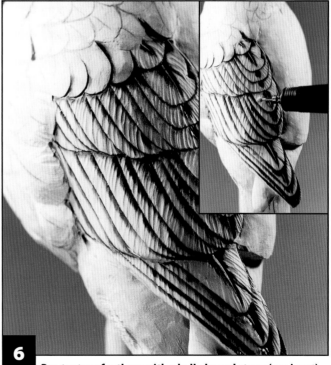

6 **Pre-texture feathers with a ball-shaped stone (see inset).** This gives shape and initiates motion in the feathers. By pre-texturing, I establish direction, feather shape, and the amount of curve the barbules will have on each feather when I burn. Don't overdo this step. Also, the pre-texture strokes don't have to be loose or numerous.

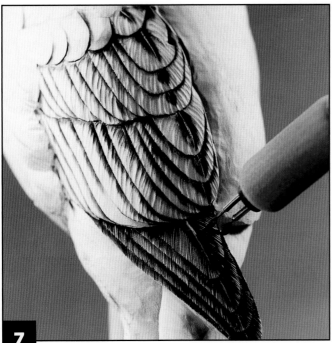

7 **Texture feathers with a straight skew burner tip.** Again, I practice on scrap wood, setting the heat at the optimum temperature for the cadence of strokes suitable to my method of burning (see Burning Tips on page 49).

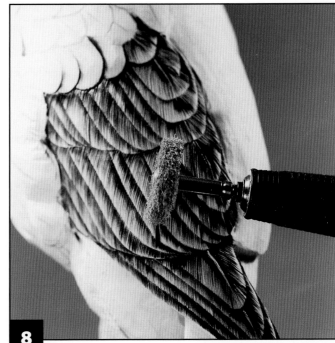

8 **Remove high spots and sharp edges.** If I observe any high spots or sharp edges that were missed in the previous step, or were created as a result of the burning, I reduce them by gently stroking with a defuzzing pad. If I apply too much pressure, I risk obliterating the texturing entirely.

Cleaning the carving

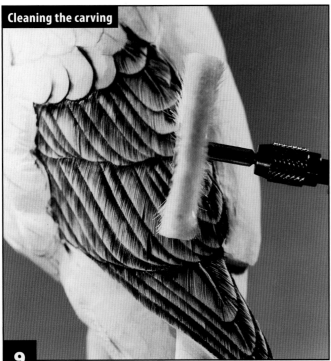

9 **Clean the textured area with a soft rotary brush.** My strokes are in the direction of the texturing to lessen any loss of texture. I use either a 1"- or 2"-diameter soft bristle brush at a low speed to achieve a nice scrubbing action. This operation is necessary before sealing and gessoing the project prior to applying the color. If any dust or wood char is left on the textured area, a small bump is created. If not removed, it will be sealed and increased in size by the gesso and the painting process. I take my carving out in harsh sunlight and turn it, looking for dirt, lumps, bumps, or any other details I may have missed.

10 **Seal the carving.** Prior to gessoing, I seal my carvings with clear matte finish automotive lacquer thinned 50% with lacquer thinner. If I run out of or can't find automotive lacquer, I use matte finish Deft, thinned with the same proportion of lacquer thinner. I use a large, soft bristle brush and let the carving absorb as much as it wants up to a usual two or three coats. I dry the surface thoroughly between coats with a hair dryer.

Texturing Strategies for Bird Carvers

By Lori Corbett

Obviously, good anatomy and having the right colors are essential to carving realistic birds, but lurking beneath the pose and paint is another key ingredient: texture.

In the early days of bird carving, carvers painted the look of texture on each bird. Then, carvers used soldering irons to capture feather anatomy. Today, micro grinders and woodburners are in every bird carver's tool kit. Once you see what grinding and burning can accomplish, you won't want to use anything else.

In the Heat of Realism

The soul of a burning unit may be the rheostat box that controls the temperature, but the heart is the tip. Pictured at right are seven burning pen tips:

1. **Angled blade with a rounded heel.** My favorite tip, it is excellent for making short, fine lines on areas such as head feathers.

2. **Extended curved blade.** It's a great choice for tight, round areas represented in the cape-to-neck transition on waterfowl.

3. **Spear pen.** My preferred tip for helping to undercut primary feathers.

4. **Scribe point.** I use this one to sign my name.

5. **Angled blade ³⁄₁₆" wide.** It can't be beat for long, sweeping feathers, and it is my second favorite tip.

6. **Bent angled blade.**

7. **Bent angled blade with rounded heal.** Both this and the previous tip I bent myself to reach under raised feathers, such as primaries. The bend allows me to keep the knife-like edge of the tip at a 90° angle to my burning surface. Because I am right-handed, the tips are bent to the right (see lower left photo). Southpaws need to bend the tips in the opposite direction.

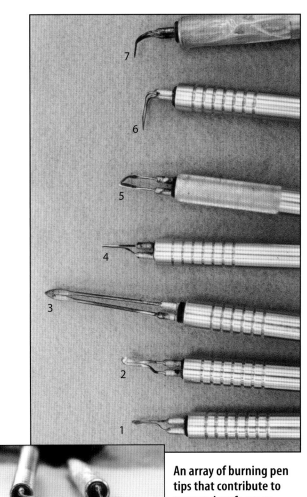

An array of burning pen tips that contribute to textured surfaces on wildfowl.

Scratch It? Sand It!

Thorough sanding is the most important preparation you can accomplish prior to grinding and burning. Any scratches left on the wood will show through the subsequent texturing and painting. My sanding strategy is as follows: The first step is an overall sanding with a small rotary drum attachment in either a flexible shaft machine or a micro grinder. I then use cloth-backed sandpaper—Swiss Red is ideal—starting with 80 or 100 grit and working through 120-, 150-, 220-, 320- and finally 500-grit paper. I make sure to sand in the direction of the grain as much as possible.

When using grits that are 220 or finer, I don't apply too much pressure because even fine paper can leave scratches. To get rid of unwanted marks, I start the sanding process over, beginning with a coarse grit such as 120.

Making Stiff, Soft, and Intermediate Feathers

Figure 1 illustrates the parts of a feather with which you should be familiar. The backbone of a feather is its shaft. Individual structures called barbs emerge from both sides of the shaft. Collectively the barbs are called vanes.

There are generally three types of feathers found on all birds, in addition to specialty feathers.

1. **Major flight feathers**–their edges are very definite and have a smooth, hard look to them.

2. **Soft feathers**—usually found on the belly, flanks, sides, head, and sometimes the breast. They are often bunched, and their shapes will vary greatly.

3. **Intermediate feathers**–fall somewhere in between the hard and soft feathers and typically make up the scapulars, back, cape coverts—both wing and tail—and sometimes the breast. They have a definite edge as the stiff feathers have, but the edges are somewhat closer, although not nearly as close as the soft feathers (see **Figure 2**).

Two steps follow on the next page for making stiff, soft, and intermediate feathers.

Sanding supplies for smoothing surfaces in your birds include cloth-backed paper, sanding sticks, a sanding drum, and Scotch-Brite.

Figure 2

Stiff Feather
Sharp delineated edges. Holds its shape well.

Intermediate Feather
Holds its shape but edges are softer than the stiff feathers.

Soft Feather
Soft and whispy edges, sometimes furlike, such as on the breast and belly of raptors.

Figure 1: Anatomy of a Feather

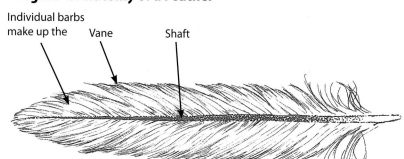

Individual barbs make up the Vane   Shaft

1 **Layout the basic outlines.** The photo shows, clockwise from the upper right, a stiff, an intermediate, and a soft feather. Notice the slight S curves of the pencil lines. The curves become longer and more sweeping as the feathers get increasingly softer.

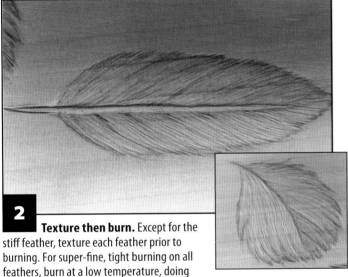

2 **Texture then burn.** Except for the stiff feather, texture each feather prior to burning. For super-fine, tight burning on all feathers, burn at a low temperature, doing little more than scoring the wood. Burned wood should be a golden brown color. For the soft feather, the texturing and burning extend unevenly past the initial outline. On an actual carving, this texture extends into the underlying feathers. For the intermediate feather, the texturing and burning do not extend as far past the outline, giving the feather an even edge, a trait of stiff feathers.

Laying Out Feather Groups

Unless you intend to carve an individual feather for display or ornamentation, you need to look at a bird in terms of feather groups. How you lay out these groups is just as important as how you texture them. A common mistake is to draw them all the same size as well as evenly spaced. I call this problem "soldiering." The feathers line up in neat rows like soldiers at attention. In **Figure 3**, you can see two groups of breast feathers. The group on the left is soldiered. The group on the right has a more pleasing flow because the feathers vary in size and direction. Yet, they still follow the flow pattern of the overall breast feather group.

Feather flow is also affected by the fact that birds are continually losing feathers and new ones are growing in to replace them. If feathers are out of place or there are small variations of shape, they appear to flow in a different direction from their neighbors. Softer feather groups tend to flow in bunches. How much depends on the species and feather group. On a waterfowl, the breast feathers bunch up less than the looser side pocket feathers, for example. On some birds of prey, the breast and belly feathers are long and soft, so the bunching is more apparent. By laying out feather groups with this kind of variation, you are adding more interest and realism to your carving. Even groups that do tend to fall into orderly rows, such as the scapular and cape feathers, will benefit from a little variation in feather size and flow.

I recommend eight steps for texturing a breast area with both short and long feathers. The instructions here include feather flow, sanding, power carving individual feathers, and burning.

Figure 3

Flow Lines
Even though the feathers follow the flow lines, they're too orderly and boring.

Flow Lines
These feathers are less orderly, sized differently, and oriented in different directions, yet still follow the flow lines.

Figure 4

Straight texturing lines. Wrong.

C curve texturing lines. Note how the direction of the barbs vary slightly from one feather to the next.

Texturing the Breast Area

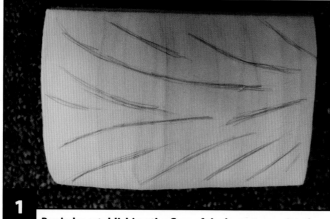

1   **Begin by establishing the flow of the breast area.** It is the direction in which the feathers grow as a group. Draw the flow lines with a graphite pencil.

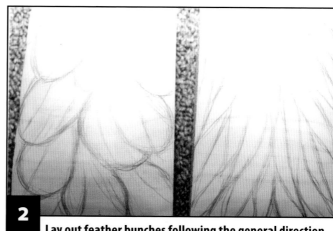

2   **Lay out feather bunches following the general direction of the flow lines.** For the short, soft feathers on the left, these bunches resemble teardrops. On long, soft feathers, the bunches resemble flames.

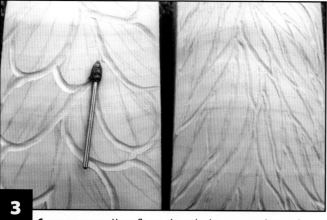

3   **Carve grooves.** Use a flame-shaped ruby carver or diamond bit to carve along these lines to form a groove. Make them shallower on the short, soft feather bunches and deeper on the longer, looser feather bunches. The process is called landscaping because hills and valleys, also called lumps and bumps, are created. Blend the bunches by using the same carving bit to knock off the hard edges of the grooves and create gentle depressions from one bunch to another. Do not leave hard edges that look like steps. After sanding them smooth, redraw the flow lines.

4   **Fill in the feathers.** Treating each bunch separately, draw the individual feathers, following the flow lines. In the case of the long, fur-like feathers on the right, draw smaller flame shapes. Make the feathers different sizes, but do not vary them too greatly. Occasionally draw one out of place, flowing in a direction slightly different from its neighbors. When done, step back and look at the overall layout. Adjust anything that appears to "soldier." Note that each bunch has its own varying flow pattern that is slightly different from the others, yet it still follows the overall flow of the major grouping.

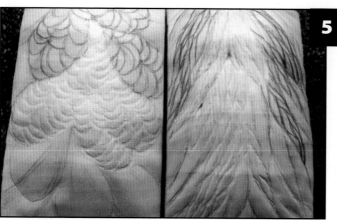

5   **Grind the feathers.** For the group on the left, use a blunt tapered diamond bit on its side to grind in the individual feathers. Work from the bottom bunch to the top bunch. Within each bunch, work from bottom feather to top feather. For the group on the right, use a flame-shaped ruby carver or a diamond bit. Then, use a ball-nose diamond bit to knock down the hard edges, making smooth, soft bumps. Notice the V-shaped areas at the intersection of some feather groups. Each is a great place to add interest. Using a small, long-tapered diamond bit, relieve the area in the point of the V and blend it out to the feather edge. Incise the V and run it under the edges of the adjacent and overlapping feathers to "raise" them slightly. Sand first with a soft-backed sanding drum using light pressure; then, hand sand with the various grits mentioned earlier for texture preparation. On the short, soft feather bunches, you want to almost sand away the individual feathers, but not quite to the point where they disappear.

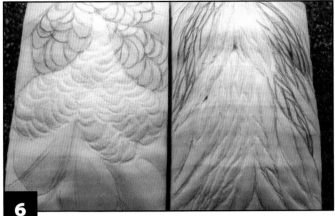
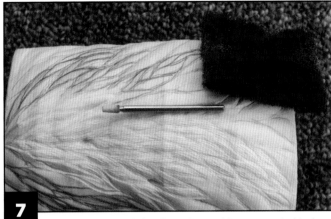

6 **Redraw the individual feathers.** For the second-to-last step prior to burning, redraw the individual feathers in the short, soft feather groups. Using a blue cone-shaped stone, grind in the feather barbs, varying their direction slightly. Use quick strokes to help maintain a light touch. Instead of making the barbs straight, grind them with small C-shaped curves (see **Figure 4**). Using a Scotch-Brite pad, lightly go over the texturing. Follow the direction of the barbs to knock off the sharp edges caused by the stone.

7 **Finish the long soft feathers.** Using a blue stone, grind in the feather barbs. Work from the outside of the feather in toward its center, following the contours (see **Figure 5**). Grind quickly, being careful not to apply too much pressure. Use the Scotch-Brite pad as you did in the previous step.

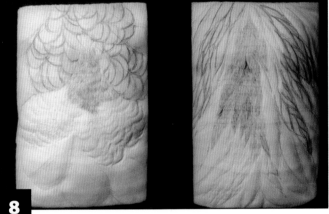

8 **Burn in the texture, following the direction of the ground-in barbs.** Use a low-temperature setting to prevent a deep burn. The result should be no darker than a golden brown. For short feathers, use an angled blade with a rounded heel. For longer, looser feathers use an angled blade ³⁄₁₆" wide. Areas are left unburned for comparison. In some cases, it may be preferable not to burn at all—for example, the breast and belly of some birds of prey. Instead, seal the wood, and then paint after texturing. Leaving the area unburned creates a looser, softer texture.

The techniques used for the short, soft feathers can be applied to the larger soft feathers such as on the side pockets of waterfowl. The major difference is that instead of teardrop-shaped bunches, you draw long sweeping S curves and lay out the feathers between them (see **Figure 6**).

Making the Difference

Study your reference material—study skins, photos, live birds—as closely as you can to determine the kinds of feathers you are looking at. When you have a feel for the types, experiment with bunching feathers. When you have the techniques mastered, your carvings will progress to a new level of realism.

Figure 5

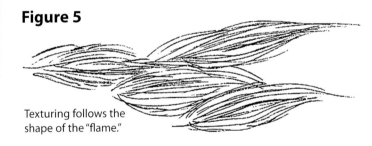

Texturing follows the shape of the "flame."

Figure 6

Flow lines as S curves.

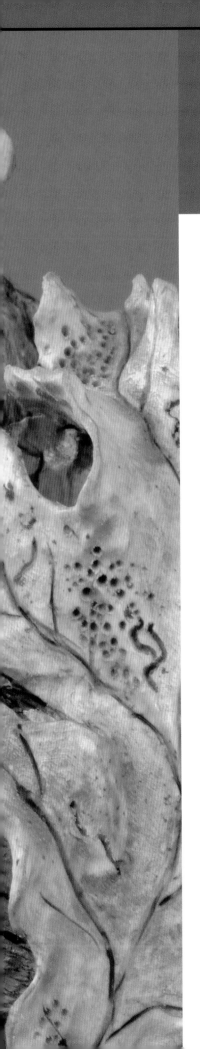

Projects

The projects featured in this section are meant to allow you to practice the techniques shown earlier in the book and to provide you with an array of projects that can be done by carving with power. Hopefully, they will get you started in power carving generally, encourage you to try a different category of carving if you're already carving with power, or inspire you to design your own creations. Projects are ordered by difficulty.

Carving Realistic Habitats, by
David Sabol, page 144.

Santa Caricature

By Frank Russell

This Santa was carved as a mantel piece (the original was about 14" high). It is dedicated to all of us who have experienced the joy of eating the cookies and milk left out by loving (and expectant!) little hands.

The mittens—one with a glass of milk, the other with a chocolate chip cookie—are more easily carved separately, and then inserted into the sleeves of the coat, allowing for greater detail around and behind the mittens, milk, cookie, and furred sleeve edges.

Photocopy to desired size

Materials & Tools

Materials:
- Wood of choice
- Acrylic paints—see painting schedule on page 64
- 5-minute epoxy glue

Tools:
- Band saw or scroll saw
- Small and medium flame-shaped carbide burs
- Small and medium flame-shaped ruby carvers
- Safe-end long taper ruby carver
- Small bud-shaped ruby carver
- Very small ball-shaped diamond bit
- Small cylinder-shaped stone bit
- Small and medium inverted cone-shaped diamond bits
- Small long and small narrow flame-shaped diamond bit
- Defuzzing mandrel or rotary bristle brush

Cutting the blank

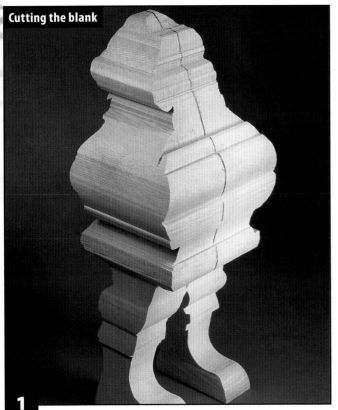

1   **Saw the project on the bandsaw.** Draw a vertical centerline all the way around the blank. A centerline is necessary to maintain symmetry during and throughout the carving sequences.

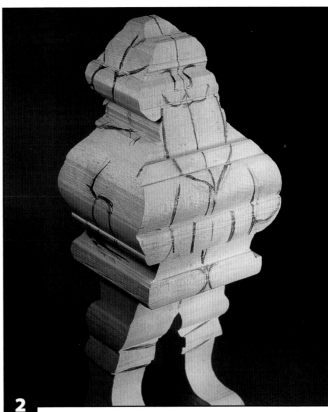

2   **Lay out all areas to be wasted away or rough shaped.** Use a small and medium flame-shaped carbide bur and a medium flame-shaped ruby carver.

Roughing cut

3   **Rough shape areas of clothing, such as the hat, coat, trousers, and boots.** Rough shape areas with hair, such as the beard, mustache, head hair, and fur trim on clothing. Use a safe-end long-taper ruby carver and small and medium flame-shaped ruby carvers.

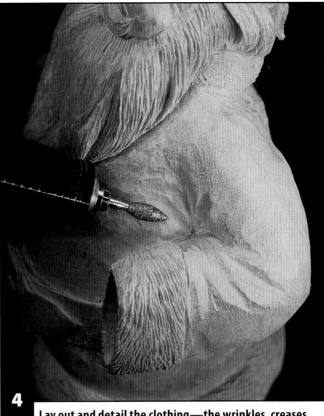

4   **Lay out and detail the clothing—the wrinkles, creases, folds, belt, belt buckle, and buttons.** Use small and medium flame-shaped ruby carvers.

5 **Lay out and shape the contours of the face.** Do the nose, eye mounds, cheeks, eyebrows, and wrinkles. Use small flame- and bud-shaped ruby carvers.

Detailing the face

6 **Detail the face.** Do the eyes and nose/nostrils and give a final touch to the wrinkles. Use the small flame-shaped ruby carver and a very small ball-shaped diamond bit.

7 **Texture all areas of hair or fur.** Use a small cylinder-shaped stone bit for eyebrows, small and medium inverted cone-shaped diamond bits and a small, long flame-shaped diamond bit for drag strokes into hair where it meets the face. Clean and defuzz the carving with a rotary bristle brush.

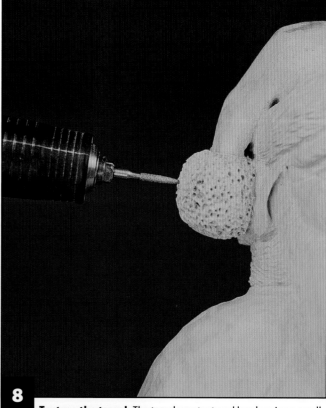

8 **Texture the tassel.** The tassel was textured by plunging a small, narrow flame-shaped diamond bit to various depths at 90° to the surface over entire tassel.

Making the arms

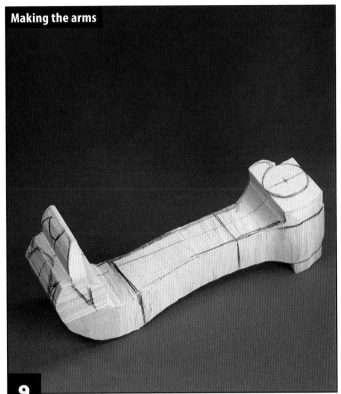

9 **Lay out and rough shape the mittens.** Both mittens were carved separately from the body and blanked out on the ends of longer pieces of stock to provide a handle for ease of carving. Use small and medium flame-shaped ruby carvers.

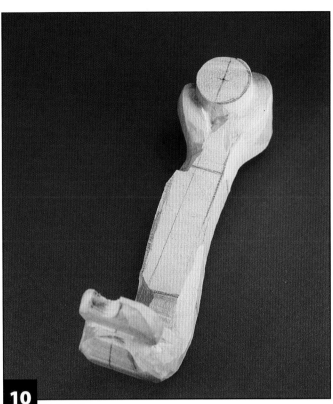

10 **Finish shape the mittens, cookie, and milk.** Use a small flame-shaped ruby carver.

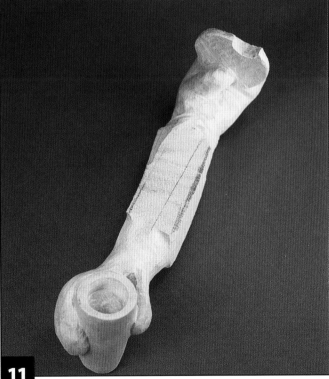

11 **Detail the mittens, cookie, and milk.** Create wrinkles and do the crumbs/chips on the cookie. Finish the depth of milk in the glass with the safe-end tapered ruby carver. Use the small flame-shaped ruby carver elsewhere.

12 **Texture the mittens with a knit stitch.** The stitch effect is accomplished by laying out the direction of the knitting with pencil, and then touching a small inverted diamond bit to the surface in opposing rows of 45° angles, which come together to form a 90° V. Clean and defuzz the mittens with a rotary bristle brush.

Painting Schedule

Trousers, Coat, and Hat

Cover all clothing with a base coat. Then, wet blend shade areas, such as creases, areas of depth, or areas where fur meets cloth. Highlight all high areas—tops of creases and large raised or exposed areas by wet blending into base color.

Base: Grumbacher red.

Shade: Burnt umber.

Highlight: Cadmium red light.

Fur Trim on Boots, Trousers, Coat, Hat, and Tassel

Mix color to medium gray and shade edges of trim bringing blended color to a very light gray in center. For the tassel, mix color to medium grey and shade bottom of tassel (where it meets red) bringing blended color to very light grey at top of tassel. Highlight fur and tassel with pure titanium white.

Base: Mars black/raw umber with titanium white.

Highlight: Titanium white.

Tassel Base: Mars black/raw umber with titanium white.

Boots and Belt

Cover boots with base color. Then, highlight creases, heels, and toes by wet-blending a touch of highlight. I always leave areas such as belts and belt buckles to paint last because they are usually parts that come into contact with my holding hand most frequently as I paint the carving.

Base: Mars black/raw umber.

Highlight: Titanium white.

Belt buckle: Base of metallic gold with wet blend of burnt sienna shade on edges.

Face, Flesh

Cover face (exclude inner eyes) with base. Blend very light touches of shade into wrinkles and on low points, and a very small amount of highlight on cheeks and tip of nose.

Base: Cadmium red medium, cadmium yellow medium, and titanium white mixed to desired flesh tone.

Shade: Burnt umber.

Highlight: Cadmium red medium.

Eyes

Paint eye white, iris, pupil, and then highlight dot. Make sure eyes are symmetrical from side to side, and ensure that irises, pupils, and highlight dots match each other in size and location. Highlight dots can be placed with a Rosemalling tool or a toothpick end.

Iris: Ultramarine blue/titanium white with a touch of raw umber.

Whites and highlight dots: Titanium white with a touch of raw umber.

Pupil: Mars black/raw umber.

Hair, Eyebrows, Beard, and Mustache

Cover all hair and beard with a medium light mixture of base. Shade bottoms of hair/beard separations by wet blending with darker tone, bringing blended color to very light gray on upper contours of the hair/beard. Highlight with pure titanium white.

Base and Shade: Payne's gray/titanium white.

Highlight: Titanium white.

Chocolate chip cookie

Cover cookie with base, wet blend edges with shade. Chocolate chips are pure raw umber.

Base: Burnt sienna/ burnt umber, touch of titanium white.

Shade: Raw umber.

Glass of milk

Paint exterior of glass with milk color up to milk level line on outside of glass. Paint interior milk, then wash entire glass (inside and out), with a transparent wash of ultramarine blue except exposed milk inside of glass.

Milk: Titanium white with a touch of raw umber.

Glass: Ultramarine blue.

Mittens

Cover mittens with base, and then wet blend shade areas, such as creases, areas of depth, or areas where mitten meets glass or cookie. Highlight all high areas—tops of creases and large areas on front of mittens. Dry thoroughly.

Attach mittens into sleeves with 5-minute epoxy. Let cure for at least an hour after initial 5-minute set. Wash with a thin antiquing coat of raw umber/water to accentuate depressions. Give attention to indentations of hair, fur trim, and knit stitching on mittens. An antiquing wash is fine for hiding tiny painting errors in depths where different colors meet, but beware of coming to rely on antiquing to cover sloppiness and/or haste.

Base: Grumbacher red.

Shade: Burnt umber.

Highlight: Cadmium red light.

Contemporary Primitive Loon Decoy

By Frank Russell

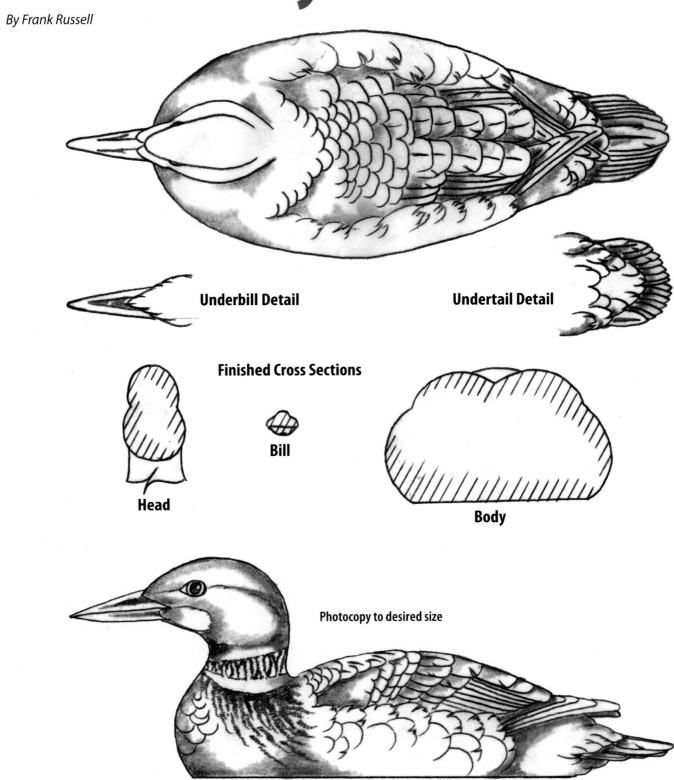

Underbill Detail

Undertail Detail

Finished Cross Sections

Head

Bill

Body

Photocopy to desired size

Materials & Tools

Materials:
- Wood of choice
- Screw, eyebolt, and waterproof glue
- Glass eye (optional)
- Paints and sealer of choice
- Glass enamel or lacquer
- Raw umber acrylic paint for antiquing wash (optional)
- Paste furniture polish with color and soft cloth

Tools:
- Band saw or scroll saw
- Small and medium flame-shaped carbide burs
- Medium and large flame-shaped ruby carvers
- Medium bud-shaped ruby carver
- 1" and ½" sanding mandrels with 200-grit paper and defuzzing mandrel
- Propane torch
- Coarse and fine steel wool and coarse cloth

Roughing out

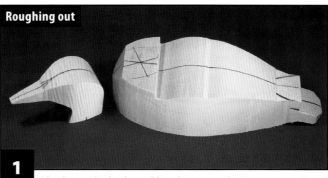

1 **Blank out the body and head separately.** Draw a vertical centerline completely around each piece. Carve the head separate from the body—a piece is unwieldy while carving the head with a body attached or vice-versa.

2 **Rough shape the head and body.** Use small and medium flame-shaped carbide burs.

For years I made Contemporary Primitives for home and workplace decoration. At one point, I was carving 32 different shorebirds, waders, and waterfowl with virtually no time for anything else.

One of the more important aspects to carving a primitive is the antiquing process which makes the carving look old, used, and aged. To make them look authentic, I actually took many of my decoy reproductions out in a field and shot at them from a distance with number 6 shot to make them look as though they had been shot over (and into) on the water.

Contemporary primitive is a term I applied to them because I wanted folks to know that they were made by modern means but using old shapes and painting patterns. Some folks actually believe them to be antiques until I explain that they were made a week ago!

Defining the feather groups

3 **Lay out and shape major feather group areas on the body.** Do the cape, side pockets, breast, back, wing coverts, wings, tail coverts, and tail. Lay out and shape contours of the head—bill, jowls, cheeks (auricular area), eye holes, top of head, and neck. For decorative purposes, I use glass eyes. For gunning purposes, I usually carve the eyes because extreme temperatures, moisture, and hard use often cause glass eyes to loosen and the wood or filler material around them to crack. Use medium and large flame-shaped ruby carvers.

4 **Join the head to the body in the desired position and glue.** I usually run a long screw up through a predrilled and countersunk hole through the body into the head because it acts as a clamp while the waterproof glue dries. For a working decoy, an eyebolt for the anchor line through the keel, body, and into the head serves the same purpose.

5 **Smooth out the carving.** Smooth out the body/head joint and the body and head, and lay out a few representative feathers in conspicuous areas along the back and sides. Shape and smooth all feathered areas. Use medium flame-shaped and medium bud-shaped ruby carvers and 1" and ½" sanding mandrels with 200-grit paper. Defuzz with a defuzzing mandrel.

6 **Char the decoy.** Using a propane torch, burn random locations around the head and body to different degrees. Avoid glue joints! Clean the decoy with fine steel wool or a large defuzzing mandrel and wipe off residue with a coarse cloth.

7 **Install the eyes if glass eyes are to be used.** Then, seal and paint as desired. For a "primitive," the old Bayman style of painting without a great amount of fine feather detail is used—just representative color patterns, so that "a mallard looks like a mallard" at a distance. There is very little blending, highlighting, shading, or feather detailing. If eyes are carved, paint them the desired color (red for a loon, with a black pupil), and coat them with several coats of glass enamel or lacquer.

8 **Distress or age the painted piece with coarse steel wool in random locations.** Don't overdo it. Dents can be added (optional) with a blunt edge implement like a pipe, a solid rod, or even the edge of a rounded bench. Add whatever scratches or dents you desire, depending on how used or aged you want the piece to look. This is also a good way to hide some painting flaws! Stay away from the eyes at all times.

9 **Flow an antiquing fluid over the entire piece.** Allow the fluid to lie in indentations, feather group separations, scratches, and dents. Wipe off high areas and dry the decoy with a hair dryer if you are using acrylic paints. I make an antiquing fluid by mixing raw umber with lots of water. You want an earth color that looks like the dirt and grime that accumulates with age and misuse. Repeat with washes until the desired antiquing color depth is acquired. Allow it to dry completely.

10 **Apply a generous coat of paste furniture polish with color.** Allow it to dry; then, vigorously buff the high points, leaving the indentations and low areas dull. I use an old athletic sock to polish. By keeping my fingers stiff, I can avoid polishing the low areas and buff only the high areas.

Woods Wizard Cypress Knee

By Frank Russell

Materials & Tools

Materials:
- Cypress knee of choice
- Clear satin finish lacquer
- Paste wax and soft cloth

Tools:
- Flame-shaped bit
- Flame-shaped ruby carver
- Cylindrical bit
- Inverted cone bit
- Flame-shaped diamond bit
- Small ball-shaped bit
- Rotary bristle brush or old toothbrush

Drawing the face

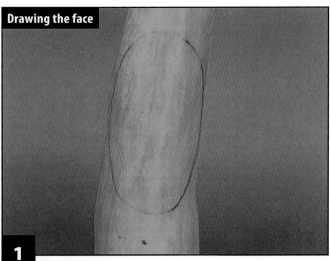

1 **Draw the face shape.** Lightly draw an egg shape the size of the face that you feel would fit on the particular surface you are about to carve. This is only a guide and will not be cut around. Once you get proficient at carving faces in this manner, you will be able to visualize a properly sized egg shape without drawing it on the carving surface.

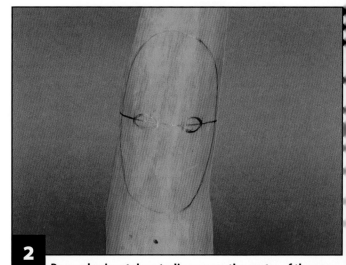

2 **Draw a horizontal centerline across the center of the egg.** This represents the line of the eyes. Divide this line into five equal parts, and draw eye shapes (twice as wide as high) in the second and fourth spaces. You will lose these eye shapes shortly, but it will give you an idea as to conformation as you begin.

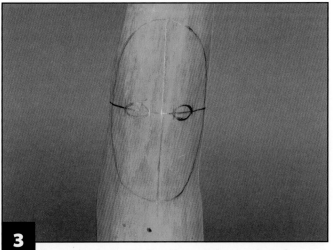

3 **Draw a vertical centerline through the egg shape from top to bottom.**

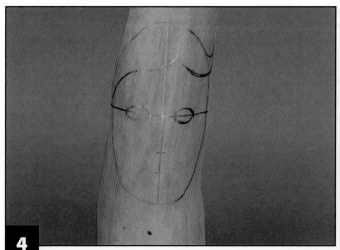

4 **Draw flowing S lines running to either side of the egg from the top central portion of the egg.** The portion above the eye line and brows will be the forehead, and these S lines represent hair that will be flowing from a separation or part beginning at the top of the head and curling outward on the forehead to the temple zone. This hair will lie atop the beard and provides excellent opportunity to carve curls, overlays, and divisions of hair during a later operation.

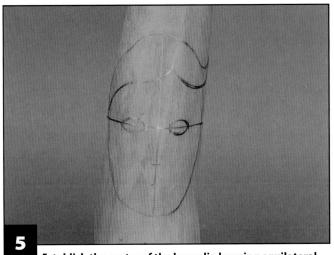

5 **Establish the center of the lower lip by using equilateral triangles.** Find the center of the lower lip by forming an equilateral triangle using the distance between the outer corners of the eyes as the legs. The bottom of the nose is found one eye length above this point.

Carving the nose

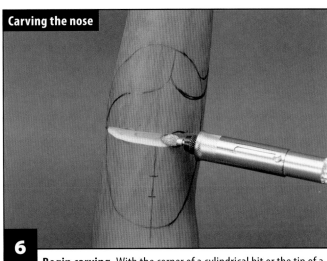

6 **Begin carving.** With the corner of a cylindrical bit or the tip of a flame-shaped bit, cut a furrow along the horizontal centerline to a depth that will satisfy, shaping the slope of the nose outward to the tip. Bit size will depend on the size of the face you are carving.

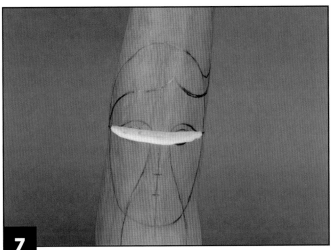

7 **Draw the nose.** Draw an arched line for the bottom of the brow. Continue the line along the outer edge of the nose. Finish the line by sweeping it however you want the mustache to flow. Carefully draw a line that matches the shape, symmetry, and distance from the vertical centerline on the other side of the face.

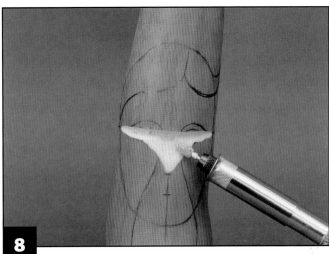

8 **Shape the nose.** Shape the slope of the nose outward to a point that will satisfy.

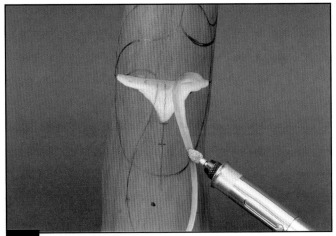

9 **Cut one line.** Using a draw stroke with a flame-shaped bit, cut along one line to a shallow depth. Greater depth will be necessary along the sides of the nose and at the outer corners of the eye.

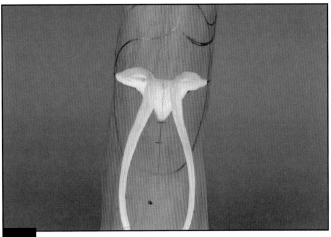

10 **Cut in the opposite line.** Observe symmetry—the shape of the brows, nose, and mustache will be controlled by these two cuts.

Shaping the eyes and nose

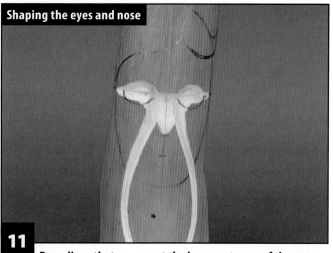

11 **Draw lines that represent the lower extreme of the eye mounds.** This line will enclose an area large enough to include the entire lower lid.

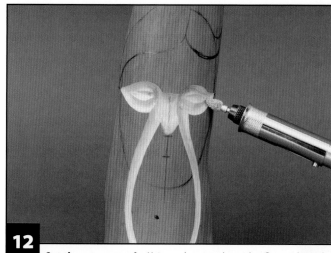

12 **Cut the eye mounds.** Using a draw stroke with a flame-shaped bit, cut along both lines to a depth that will satisfy the shallowest contours along the line. (The most forward portion of the eye mound.)

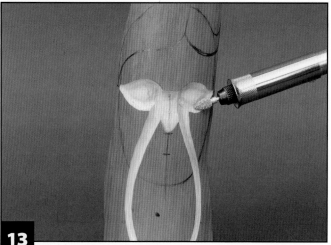

13 **Continue to rough shape eye mounds, maintaining a symmetrical shape for both.** Deepen the inner corners of the eye mounds where they blend into the bridge of the nose, and allow the outer end of the mound to blend into the temple area.

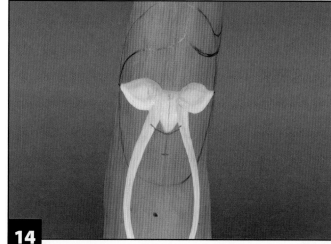

14 **Draw the shallow V shape of the tip of the nose.** Beware making this V too sharp, as it will govern the overall shape of the nose. I suggest a slope of about 15°. It is advisable to make the V shallow to begin with—it can always be sharpened.

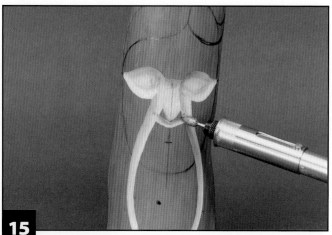

15 **Cut the nose V.** Use an inverted cone or a flame-shaped bit held at a high angle. Use care not to cut too deeply, as the mustache will be running up underneath the nose, and stock should be left for it.

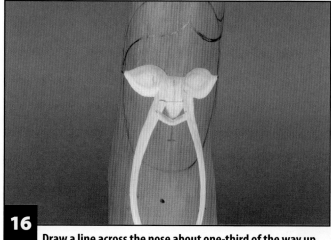

16 **Draw a line across the nose about one-third of the way up from the tip.** This line will locate the wings of the nose, so make sure the line is at a 90° angle to the vertical centerline, and the outer extremes are equal.

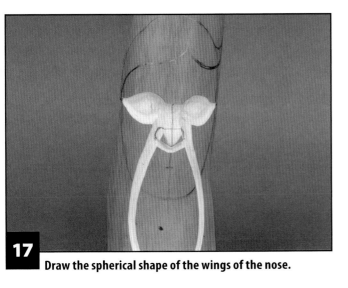

17 **Draw the spherical shape of the wings of the nose.**

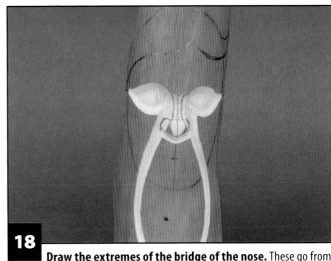

18 **Draw the extremes of the bridge of the nose.** These go from the brow line down and around the ball of the nose.

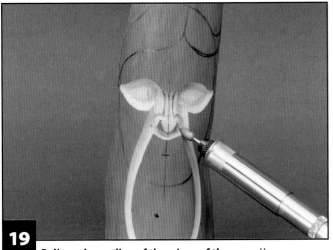

19 **Relieve the outline of the wings of the nose.** Use a flame-shaped bit held at a high angle. Begin at the bottom, along the wing line, and finish with an angle at the bridge line.

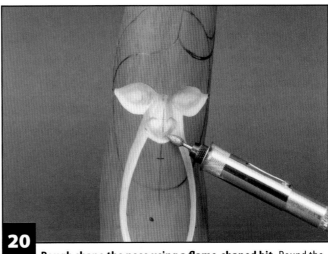

20 **Rough shape the nose using a flame-shaped bit.** Round the wings of the nose and blend gently into the ball of the nose. Use care, but remove any sharp edges. There are no sharp corners on the nose.

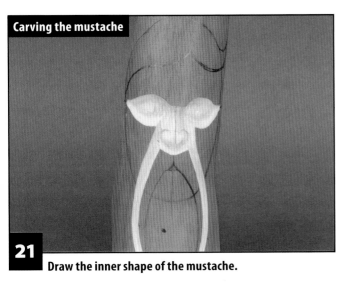

Carving the mustache

21 **Draw the inner shape of the mustache.**

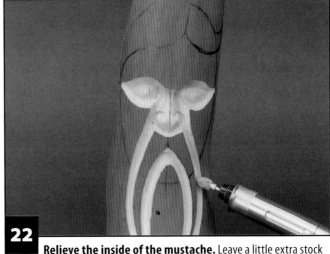

22 **Relieve the inside of the mustache.** Leave a little extra stock where the two inner sides of the mustache come together over the mouth. This extra stock will later become the lower lip.

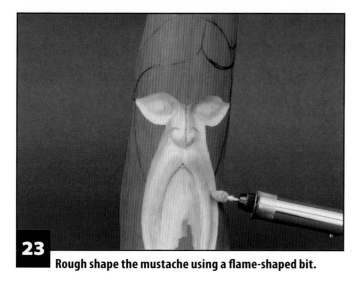

23 Rough shape the mustache using a flame-shaped bit.

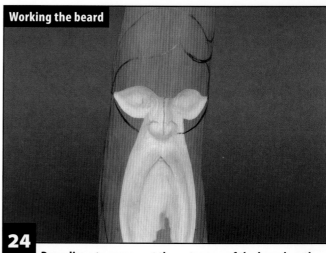

Working the beard

24 Draw lines to represent the extremes of the beard on the cheeks. They go from the temple area down to the mustache just slightly below the nose.

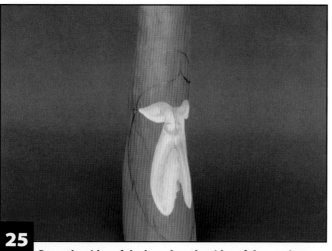

25 Draw the sides of the beard on the sides of the carving surface. They are below where the ears would be. Give thought to the fullness, thinness, curliness, direction of hair flow, etc., that you want your beard to have.

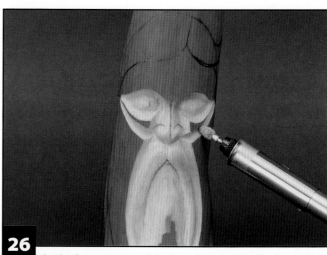

26 Cut in the extremes of the beard on the cheeks. Be sure to use care in this area.

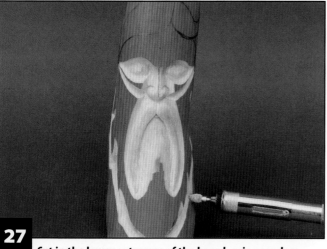

27 Cut in the lower extremes of the beard, using random flowing drag strokes with a flame-shaped bit. These go from the area below the curls of the forehead hair down to the beard tip.

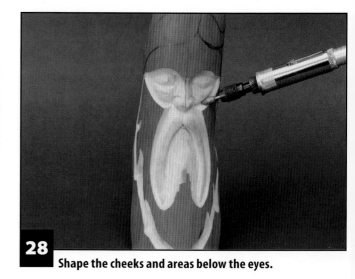

28 Shape the cheeks and areas below the eyes.

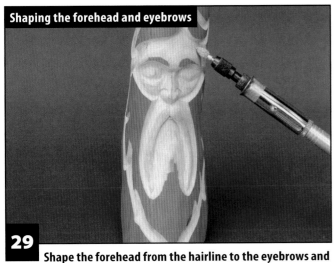

29 **Shape the forehead from the hairline to the eyebrows and into the temples.** Undercut hair as necessary to raise it away from the skin. Leave a bit of extra stock in the area of the eyebrows to relieve away the size and shape of eyebrows that you want.

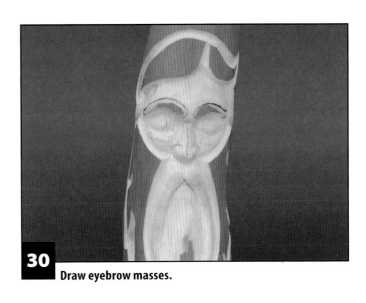

30 **Draw eyebrow masses.**

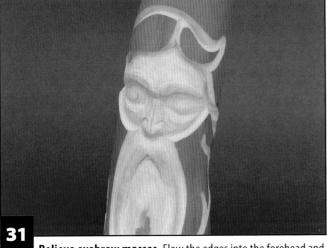

31 **Relieve eyebrow masses.** Flow the edges into the forehead and lower brow arches.

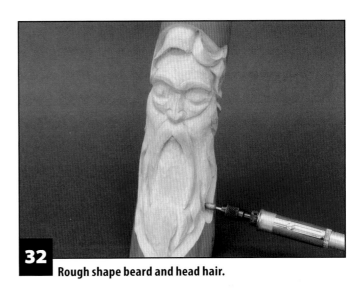

32 **Rough shape beard and head hair.**

Completing the eyes

33 **Re-establish the eye centerline and draw the finished shape of eyes.** Remember the location the eyes were drawn within. Make sure both eyes are the same size and precisely located. Nothing will spoil this carving quicker than having misshapen or mislocated eyes.

34 **Carve the eyes.** Give expression, such as turning the corners up slightly to make the eyes happy,

Completing the nose

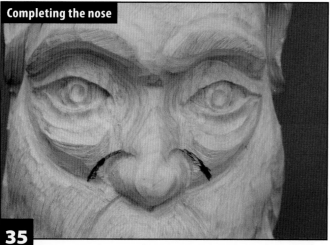

35 **Draw matching nasolabial folds (smile lines).** These are the distinct creases that start from the tops of the nose wings and head toward the corners of the mouth. They will terminate at the point where they intersect the top of the beard.

36 **Cut nasolabial folds in with a flame-shaped ruby carver.** Hold it at a 45° angle. Round and blend sides of folds. Finish shaping the cheeks, tear ducts, and temples as necessary with a flame-shaped ruby carver.

37 **Draw the extreme of the exposed lower lip and shape opening of the mouth under the mustache.** Use a flame-shaped ruby carver. For smaller faces, a smaller flame-shaped diamond bit will make the operation easier.

38 **Draw and cut the nostrils.** The nostrils are shaped like opposing commas. Cut them using a small ball-shaped bit for the body (hole) and a small flame-shaped bit for the tail of the nostril that curls up to disappear under the nose wing.

Creating wrinkles

39 **Draw wrinkles as desired.** Put them at the corners of the eyes, forehead, center brow, and below the eyes. Make sure you like what you have drawn both in shape and in number before you cut them in.

40 **Relieve wrinkles with a flame-shaped bit.** Smooth the edges of the wrinkles so they won't appear exaggerated.

Finishing the hair

41 **Evaluate all areas of hair and draw any additional hair details.** These can be curls, separations, overlays, and raised areas.

42 **Finish the shaping.** Relieve all details, finish shape details, and smooth out all areas of hair in preparation for texturing.

43 **Draw flow lines over each area of hair.** These areas are the head hair, eyebrows, mustache, and beard. Hold the carving at arm's length and decide that all the hairlines flow as you want them to.

44 **Texture all areas of hair starting at the bottom of each area and working upward.** No matter what scale of hair you decide on, either an inverted cone shape or cylinder shape bit is ideal for texturing. I find either bit gives essentially the same result. For coarser hair, use an aggressive (coarse) larger bit, and for finer hair, use a smaller finer grit bit.

Cleaning and sealing the carving

45 **Clean all areas with a rotary brush or a defuzzing pad.** Use care—work in the direction of the texture and use a low rpm or you risk losing the texture detail. If you don't have a rotary brush, an old toothbrush can be used, though it takes a bit more effort to remove debris and fuzz.

46 **Seal the carving.** Flow a coat of thinned, clear lacquer (satin finish) over the entire piece.

47 **Coat carving with a medium-light layer of paste wax.** Buff just the high points by covering your hand with an old athletic sock and buffing with your hand held stiff.

Maple Leaf Earrings

By Kenny Vermillion,
Photography by Carl Saathoff

Not every carving has to be a complicated composition. This is a wonderful exercise for developing both power carving and painting skills. Learning new techniques can be discouraging if projects take forever to complete. Small items such as these are challenging, due to their size, while being achievable in a relatively short period of time. These earrings are also attractive and a popular sale or gift item.

Almost everything I carve is from tupelo because it has ideal qualities for wildlife subjects. These maple leaf earrings are made of scrap wood from other subjects. I have always used acrylic paint. Most of my students are intimidated by painting, but once they understand a logical approach, they usually enjoy it.

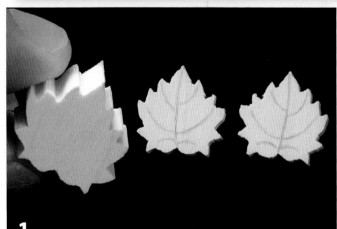

1 **Cut the blank to shape.** The blank is sawn from a select piece of wood with flat grain running from front to back with the center vein. The blank is cut in half to create two symmetrical earrings. After sawing, lightly sand the back of each leaf with fine-grit sandpaper. Draw on the leaf vein details. I use a mechanical pencil with 0.5mm HB lead. Draw lightly, because you cannot erase scribing. Curved veins are more natural and pleasing to the eye.

2 **Establish the veins with the small, pointed diamond bit.** Create shallow furrows by pulling the bit the full length of the veins. Point the bit to the center of the leaf and lightly pull toward the outside edge for better control. Do not use pressure or force the tool—merely guide the bit.

Carving the leaves

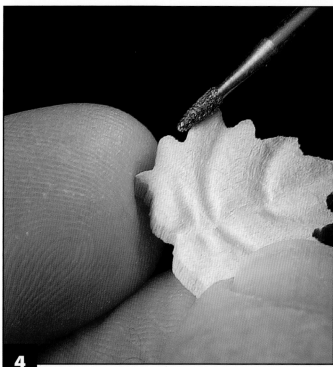

3 **Carve the remainder of the leaf top with the small flame diamond bit.** Begin to deepen and contour the veins. The center vein is shallowest in the center and deepens at each end. The side veins originate from the center vein. Gently lead the bit, execute the stroke, and follow through. Flicking creates dips instead of contours. Short strokes are easier to control than long ones. Understand where you are going before carving.

4 **Follow the rotation of the tool when carving.** Avoid stroking over the edge of the leaf that is farthest away because it will dig and run over the side. Rotate the leaf when carving on the edge. This will facilitate stroking forward from the outside toward the center. The grain will dictate whether you should orient the bit straight or diagonally.

5 **Contour the leaf by creating sweeping peaks and valleys.** Use the side of the bit and lightly stroke in the direction of the bit rotation. Pulling against the rotation sacrifices control. The outside edges are deeper in the veins and higher between them. Retain enough thickness to ensure the strength of the leaf. The veins are well-defined in the center of the leaf, and more varied toward the edges. Still using the side of the bit, it may be necessary to stroke diagonally across the grain of the wood to remove it evenly.

6 **Reduce the grit of a bonded ruby bit.** Ruby bits tend to be coarse and inconsistent. Run the bit at high speed and carefully brush it across a diamond strop. It is important to reduce the grit consistently from the hilt to the point. Frequently run the side of the bit on a scrap piece of wood to test for spikes and inconsistencies. Be careful not to remove all of the grit.

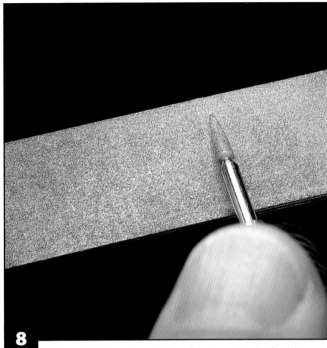

7 **Redefine the veins.** Use the reduced-grit bonded ruby bit and slowly pull the point from the center toward the edge at a high rpm. Smooth each section between the veins. Stroking diagonally across the grain will smooth it evenly.

8 **Reduce the diameter of the ruby stone.** Stroke the side on a diamond strop at moderate rpms. Use the bonding agent at the base of the stone as a guide. Do not remove the stone all the way to the shaft. Be careful—if the stone gets too hot, the bonding agent will break down and the stone will be worthless.

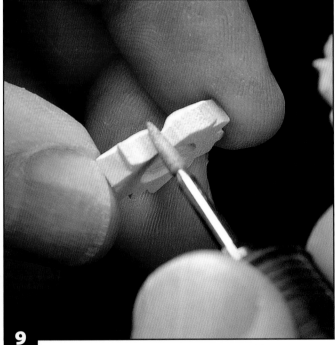

Attaching the post

9 **Lightly soften the saw marks.** Use the side of the reduced-diameter ruby stone at a high rpm, around the sides of the leaf. Hold the stone parallel to the saw marks and stroke carefully to maintain them evenly up and down the sides. Use the side of the tip of the ruby stone at a moderate rpm to lightly round the edges on both top and bottom on all sides of the leaf. Wooden 90° angles on edges chip and break.

10 **Carve a recess to accommodate the earring posts.** Center the post on the back of the earring. Hold it in place with a pencil eraser, and trace the outline with a pencil. Follow the pencil line using a small diamond ball to recess the wood the approximate thickness of the post base. Clean out the recess using slow, forward strokes for consistent depth. A flat bottom is important for the post to set squarely.

11 **Glue the post onto the earring using five-minute epoxy.**
Mix the epoxy according to the manufacturer's directions. Apply it the bottom of the post bases with a toothpick. If it strings from the toothpick, it has already begun to set up and should not be used. Use the pencil eraser to press the post base into the recess. Then, use a pencil to put your initials on the backs.

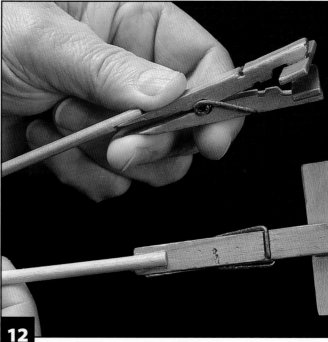

12 **Make clamps to hold the earrings.** Use five-minute epoxy to glue a notched dowel to the outside of a clothespin. Cut a popsicle stick in half and glue it to the inside of the clothespin. This gives you something to hold on to when painting. The dowels can be inserted into holes drilled in a scrap 2 x 4 to hold the clamps while the paint dries.

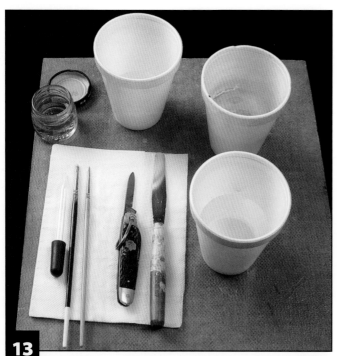

13 **Organize your painting supplies.** Set up three cups of water. One cup of water (the upper left) is for mixing with paint and must be kept clean. The other two are used to clean brushes—always do the first swishing of the brush in the same cup and the final swishing in the other. The window cleaner with ammonia in the jar is used to clean the brushes (see Cleaning Up Paintbrushes on page 85). The eyedropper is used to measure out water, and the knife and spatula are used to measure paints (see Step 15). The stiff-bristled brush is used to mix the paints, and the camel hair brush is used to apply the paint.

14 **Apply a spray lacquer.** The wood must be well-sealed to prevent the grain from rising. Apply three or four light coats to the top, sides, and bottom. Let the lacquered earrings set for at least 12 hours before painting, then peel the lacquer off of the post. Mix a few drops of white gesso with water to the consistency of milk and apply a very small amount to the tip of the camel hair brush. Wipe one side on the edge of the palette well. Paint from the center vein out, one section at a time, with as few strokes as possible. Apply the gesso to the top of the leaf only. Apply a second coat after the first coat has thoroughly dried. Even coverage is necessary.

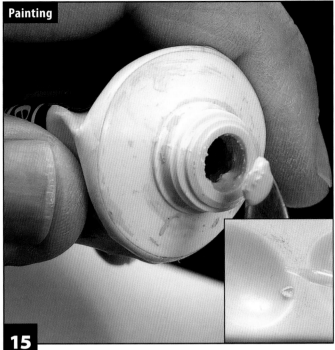

15 **Measure out a small amount of paint.** Use an old knife to scrape a small amount from the end of the tube. Wipe this paint on the side of the palette well and use the eyedropper to add a few drops of water. Dip the stiff-bristled brush in water and then mix the paint. Add water as needed to get the consistency of skim milk.

16 **Apply an even coat of yellow to the top of the leaf.** Use the camel hair brush and the same techniques you used to apply the Gesso. This is a base color coat because the paint is translucent. If one coat does not cover evenly, apply additional coats as needed. Allow each coat to dry before adding the next. To keep the paint for future use, cover the palette with a wet sponge.

Tips:

REMOVING FOREIGN MATERIAL

If you have a speck of foreign material on the surface, lift it off with the brush you are using. However, if this doesn't work, the dull knife will. Be careful to not dig into the previous coats.

RETOUCHING

Resist the temptation to retouch before the paint has dried. The paint is continually drying, so if strokes are repeatedly overlapped, the latest stroke will lift the paint from the first strokes.

TOUCH-UPS

Touch-ups can be done by touching the brush tip to the paint and then stippling or dabbing onto the leaf.

STEADY HANDS

Brace your hands together when carving the earring. Since it is so small, it is easiest to hold the earring in your hand, but even normal breathing makes it hard to hold your hands steady. Hold the power carver the same as a pencil and extend one finger to touch the hand holding the earring. That way, if your hands move, they are more likely to move together—giving you coordinated control.

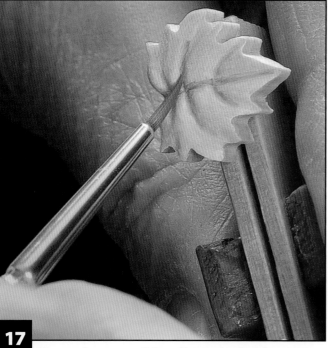

17 **Mix equal amounts of the yellow and red with water to get orange.** Use a separate palette well. Brush one coat onto the veins. This is the beginning of the build-up of color. Blending acrylic paints with only one coat is very difficult. More pleasing results are achieved with multiple thin coats that overlap or underlap. Each coat must be dry before applying the next.

18 **Swish and wipe your brush.** Touch the tip of the brush to the orange paint. Starting on the first section of the leaf, touch the point of the brush to the outside edge, next to the center vein. Hold the brush slightly on its side with the ferrule toward the section's vein, and stroke along the outside perimeter of the section. Paint each remaining section of the leaf in the same manner. The perimeters of each section should be orange and the centers should be yellow. Save this color for future use.

19 **Mix red paint with water.** Mix the same quantity as you did with the yellow (in Step 15). Stir both the red and yellow paint as both will be used. Touch the tip of the brush to the red, and paint the perimeter of the first section. Quickly wipe the brush on a paper towel, touch the tip of the brush to the yellow, and paint the center of this same section. Gently stroke where the red and yellow meet. Do not overwork it; two or three strokes should be enough. The leaf on the right shows the first coat of orange and the leaf on the left shows the red and yellow blending.

Finishing

20 **Return to the orange color.** Increase the volume by one-third with water, and stir well. This will be the homogenizing wash that ties all of the colors together. One coat should be enough. Mix burnt sienna, a very small amount of acra violet, and a couple drops of water to a consistency of thick cream. Using vertical strokes (follow the saw marks), paint the sides with this color all the way around the leaf. Too much pressure on the brush will squeeze paint onto the top and bottom of the leaf.

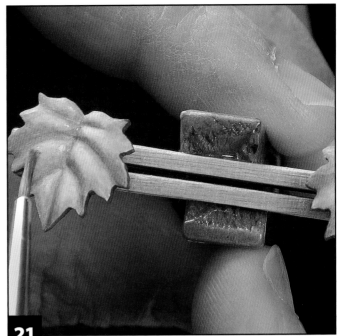

21 **Mix the gloss medium and varnish with water to the consistency of milk.** Put one coat on the top. Be careful not to get it on the sides. This establishes two finishes which adds visual interest. Put the backs on the posts to complete the earrings.

Materials & Tools

Materials:
- ⅜" x 1" x 1" tupelo
- 5-minute epoxy glue
- Earring posts and backs
- Acrylic tube paints: brilliant yellow, cadmium red light, burnt sienna, acra violet
- Interior/exterior spray lacquer
- Gesso
- Gloss medium and varnish

Tools:
- Band saw or scroll saw
- Diamond strop (medium or fine grit)
- Diamond bits (medium grit): small point, small flame, small ball
- Bonded ruby bit, small flame, fine grit
- Ruby stone bit, tapered
- Stiff-bristled brush
- Camel hair brush

Tips:

CLEANING UP PAINTBRUSHES

Ammonia is a solvent for acrylic paint and window cleaner with ammonia contains just the right amount. Occasional swishing of the brushes in window cleaner prolongs their life by cleaning the paint from the ferrules. When paint dries in the brush ferrule, the bristles splay and become brittle. Follow swishing in the window cleaner by swishing in both water cups then dragging off on the towel to complete the procedure.

Enlarge the pattern for clip-on earrings.

Photocopy at 100%

Collapsible Telescoping Rod

By Lynn Diel

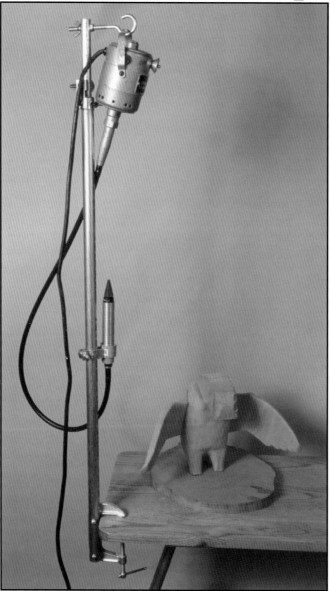

After purchasing a flexible shaft tool, I realized I would have to hang it before I could use it, which led to an engineering challenge.

For my needs, I wanted the hanger to be adjustable so that I could use it while standing or sitting. In addition, I wanted the rod to be as compact as possible to make it portable.

After scrounging around my junk boxes, I found the leg from a discarded camera tripod. It looked like it would have possibilities. After assembling the device, I attached it to my workbench, placed my flexible shaft tool on the hanger, and put it to use. Adjustment was easy because I was able to change the height by releasing one of the fasteners for the leg.

When Christmas came around, I received another flexible shaft tool. I now had two with only one hanger. I added a second hanger to the tripod leg, but I soon found I needed a stronger support. That led to my latest invention.

When designing a tool or accessory, I strive to build something that does not require a full woodworking or machine shop. This has led to strange looks from sales staff and others as I walk around hardware stores looking for parts that seem to have no logical association with my latest design.

After deciding that the major components for my collapsible telescoping rod would be conduit, I purchased 3' sections of ½"- and ¾"-diameter pipe, which made for a simple assembly. But the locking mechanism proved to be the most challenging part of the project.

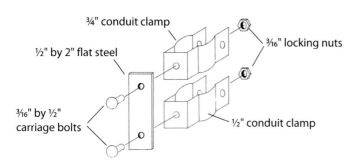

Figure 1. Base Assembly

¾" conduit clamp

½" by 2" flat steel

³⁄₁₆" locking nuts

³⁄₁₆" by ½" carriage bolts

½" conduit clamp

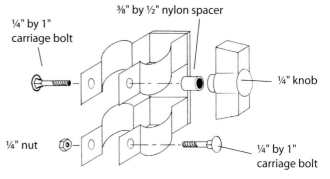

Figure 2. Threaded Knob Assembly

¼" by 1" carriage bolt

⅜" by ½" nylon spacer

¼" knob

¼" nut

¼" by 1" carriage bolt

Construction

The ½" by 2" flat steel provides the bridge that holds the two conduit holders together. Two ³⁄₁₆" carriage bolts and nuts hold the flat steel to the two conduit clamps. After putting the base assembly together (see **Figure 1**), the next step is to make the threaded knob assembly. Use carriage bolts so that the threaded knob and holding nut can be attached (see **Figure 2**). Secure the base assembly to the ¾" conduit by tightening the ¼" nut onto the ¾" conduit clamp. The base assembly on pipe is complete (see **Figure 3**).

Next, construct a slider assembly that fastens to the ½" conduit, allowing it to slide inside the ¾" conduit. The slider consists of a ¾"-diameter by 2"-long dowel. It allows the conduit to slide up and down without rattling or excessive play. Attach the dowel to the ½" conduit with epoxy glue. An alternative is to drill a small hole in the conduit and insert a nail or screw to hold the dowel in place (see **Figure 4**).

For the hook assembly, drill a ⁵⁄₁₆"-diameter hole 1" from the top of the ½" conduit, insert the ¼"-by-6"-long hook into the pipe, and tighten the two nuts (see **Figure 5**). If you want two hooks, drill a second ⁵⁄₁₆"-diameter hole 1" below the first one.

Next, slide the ½" conduit past the ½" conduit clamp and into the ¾" conduit. The telescoping rod assembly is complete (see **Figure 6**). Adjusting the rod is simple. Loosen the threaded knob and slide the bar up or down. Then, tighten the knob to lock the rod in place.

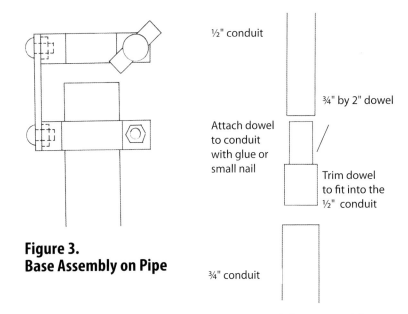

**Figure 3.
Base Assembly on Pipe**

½" conduit

¾" by 2" dowel

Attach dowel to conduit with glue or small nail

Trim dowel to fit into the ½" conduit

¾" conduit

Figure 4. Slider Assembly

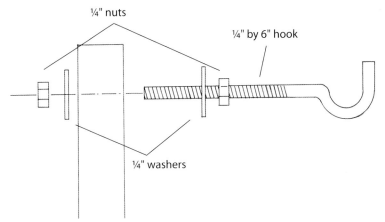

¼" nuts

¼" by 6" hook

¼" washers

Figure 5. Hook Assembly

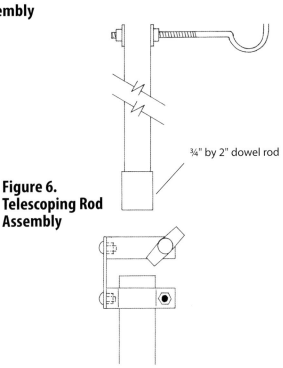

**Figure 6.
Telescoping Rod
Assembly**

¾" by 2" dowel rod

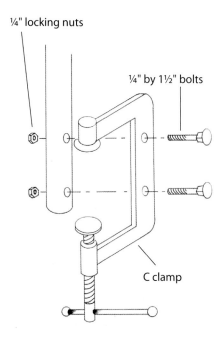

¼" locking nuts

¼" by 1½" bolts

C clamp

**Figure 7.
Clamp Assembly**

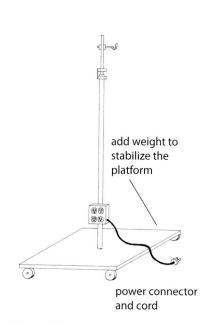

add weight to stabilize the platform

power connector and cord

**Figure 8.
Simple Base on Wheels**

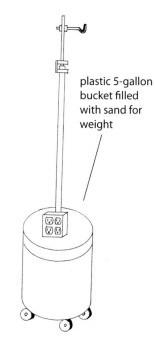

plastic 5-gallon bucket filled with sand for weight

**Figure 9.
Weighted Bucket on Wheels**

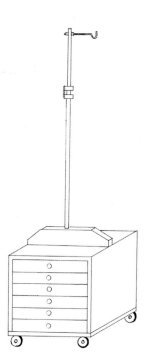

**Figure 10.
Cabinet on Wheels**

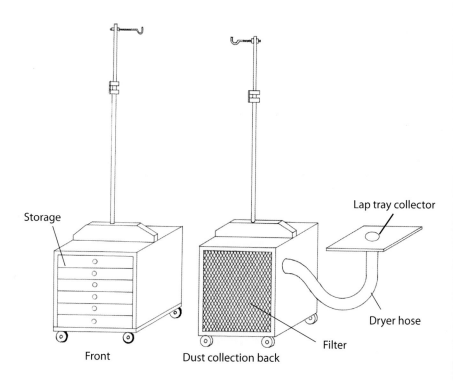

Storage

Front

Dust collection back

Filter

Lap tray collector

Dryer hose

Figure 11. Dust Collector on Wheels

To make the clamp assembly, which allows the rod to be secured to a table, drill two ⁵⁄₁₆"-diameter holes into a C-clamp and two matching holes into the ¾" conduit (see **Figure 7**). Use two ¼"-by-1½" bolts and locking nuts to secure the conduit to the C-clamp. Note: Be careful not to overtighten the nuts, which could bend the conduit.

Options

By using longer sections of conduit, a simple base on wheels can be constructed. An outlet box and power cord is incorporated into the pipe and a sandbag can be placed on the base for stability (see **Figure 8**).

An alternative is filling a five-gallon container with sand to create a weighted bucket on wheels (see **Figure 9**). A board will have to be placed on the bottom of the bucket to hold the bottom end of the conduit in place.

As I began to use my flexible shaft tool, it became evident that I would need storage for the accessories. I modified the original design to make a cabinet on wheels (see **Figure 10**) that holds bits and other components.

After finding that flexible shaft tools generate quite a lot of dust, I modified my cabinet to accommodate a small squirrel-cage fan and filter. When attached to a hose and lap tray, I have a dust collector on wheels (see **Figure 11**).

Like most carvers, I never have too many drawers for storage. I modified my cabinet on wheels by doubling its height and adding additional drawers. I also changed the holder on top to give me a cabinet with two rods (see **Figure 12**).

Figure 12.
Cabinet with Two Rods

Estimated Cost

The prices listed are what I paid at a local hardware chain store to build the basic collapsible telescoping rod with C-clamp.

Quantity	Description	Cost
2	³⁄₁₆" by ½" carriage bolts	.16
2	³⁄₁₆" locking nuts	.32
1	½" by 2" flat steel	.49
1	½" electrical conduit clamp	.75
1	¾" electrical conduit clamp	.75
1	⅜" by ½" nylon spacer	.15
2	¼" by 1" carriage bolts	.18
1	¼" nut	.08
1	¼" threaded tee knob	1.29
1	½" by 36" electrical conduit	.87
1	¾" by 36" electrical conduit	1.77
1	¾" by 2" dowel rod	.05
1	¼" by 6" hanger bolt	1.49
2	¼" washers	.04
2	¼" nuts	.08
1	C-clamp	3.49
2	¼" by 1½" bolts	.18
2	¼" locking nuts	.38
	Total	$12.52

Carve and Paint a Killdeer

By Jack Kochan

You don't have to be a professional wildfowl carver to capture the essence of an attractive shorebird like the killdeer. In the traditions of nineteenth- and early twentieth-century decoy makers who lured birds to marshes and beaches with counterfeits, the carved bird can be approached as a simple but pleasing form, shaped, sanded, and finished with nothing more than a dark shoe polish. Mount it on a stick as the old timers did, and the killdeer lends itself handsomely to a mantel or shelf instead of a shoreline.

My finished piece isn't quite so simple, but the techniques needed to bring more realism to the killdeer are not hard to master and power carving makes it all that much easier. After rounding its body, I shaped the eyes, ground in the wing outlines, turned the head, and settled for a paint application that brings out the basic colors of the bird plus a few feather details.

Tupelo, a Power Carver's First Choice

While the decoy makers of a bygone era used cedar or pine to fashion their birds, I prefer tupelo for several reasons. Being a power carver, I find tupelo and rotary tools are natural allies. Chips and dust come away from a cutout with little resistance. Because of the seemingly grainless nature of the wood—actually, it's an interlocking grain—fuzzy surfaces are not a problem. Basswood and jelutong also lend themselves to power carving, but they require a lot of extra sanding to remove wood fibers that tend to stick up like tiny hairs.

Be advised tupelo does not carve easily with hand tools. Cutting edges rely on grain direction and firmness to slice and even make stop cuts. Knives, chisels, and gouges meet a lot of resistance with tupelo's grain, and consequently the wood is often described as spongy in texture. However, tupelo has no hard and soft transitions between growth rings, unlike pine.

In my mind, the biggest advantage to using tupelo is that thin pieces resist breakage. Because of the interlocking grain, there is strength in all directions. A fragile area like the bill of the killdeer, while not completely safe from damage, won't cause as much concern as a bill carved from basswood.

Tupelo, however, is a thirsty wood that will soak up the humidity in your carving area and cause the wood to swell.

By the next morning, you may well find that the fine burning and stoning lines have lost their crispness. Sealing the wood with a thin coat of lacquer prior to turning in for the night remedies that problem.

Primed for Painting

Before opening up the paint containers or purchasing colors, take some time to study my painting notes. I sealed the bird prior to painting and applied several coats of gesso that I mixed with a flow medium. An acrylic additive, the flow medium modifies the handling properties of the paint and allows for smoother application. The gesso mix actually lends itself to one of the primary colors of the killdeer. Additional applications were required to cover the filler used at the neck joint. The rest of the colors were acrylic gouaches.

Many wildfowl carvers use gouaches because of their flat, non-glossy finish, which more closely resembles a feather's lifelike sheen. Having pigments that are more finely ground than other paints, the gouaches lend themselves well to airbrushing, and they do not fill in fine texturing details when several thin washes are applied.

I could have simplified the painting by limiting the bird to two color tones, one for the belly and the other for the head, back, and tail. But I opted to paint individual feathers on the cape and primaries, dark stripes on the breast and forehead, and a white stripe above the eyes. I even gave some color to the eyes to make them more realistic.

When mounted on a wood base, in this case a cross section of a limb from my fireplace woodpile, the killdeer is an attention getter even when viewed up close.

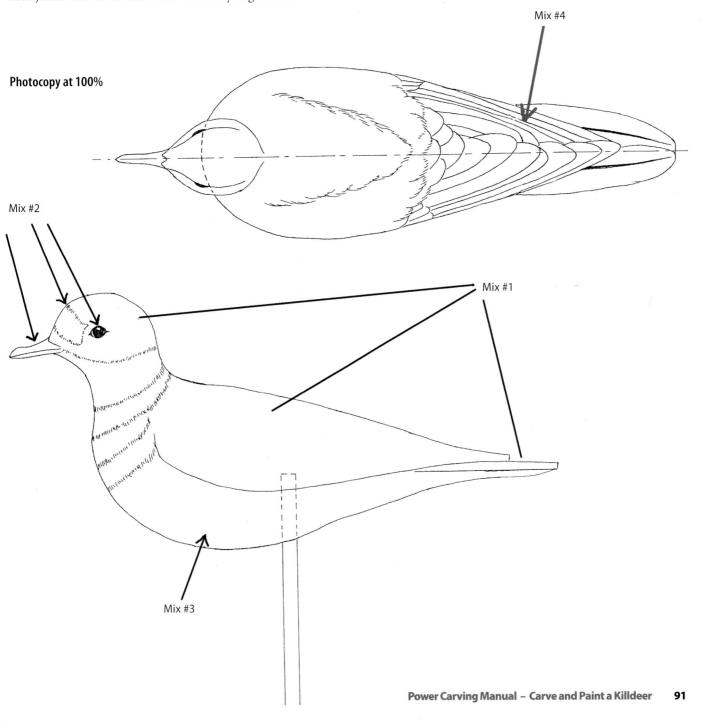

Mix #4

Photocopy at 100%

Mix #2

Mix #1

Mix #3

PAINTING AND FINISHING TIPS

PREP:

1. Sand the completed carving with cloth-backed sandpaper, starting with 120-grit, then 220-grit, then 400-grit sandpaper.

2. Seal with a 50/50 mix of lacquer and lacquer thinner. Let it dry for a minimum of four hours, then lightly sand with 400-grit sandpaper.

3. Mix gesso and 25% flow medium; brush over the entire carving. Dry with a hair dryer, then sand and apply a second coat of gesso mix. Repeat until evenly white, and set aside for 24 hours to dry.

4. Remove any fuzz on the carving by scrubbing with a clean, dry toothbrush or 400-grit sandpaper.

PAINT:

1. Use a watercolor pencil to sketch the locations of stripes on the breast, forehead, and above the eyes.

2. For the head, back, and tail, use Mix #1 (refer to swatches), add a few drops of flow medium and apply as illustrated with a #8 filbert brush. Repeat until the desired color is achieved.

3. For the black stripes, the eyes, and bill, use Mix #2; add a few drops of flow medium and apply as illustrated. Build up coats until a dark black is achieved; drag a little black onto the white areas to give the appearance of feather overlap.

4. After the eyes are dry, paint eyelids with naphthol red.

5. For the bird's underside, use Mix #3 and paint over all the white areas. Use the same mix to paint a narrow stripe over each eye.

6. Use Mix #4 and paint the primary wing feather tips using a small liner brush.

7. Let it dry for at least eight hours.

FINISH:

1. Spray the piece with a semi-gloss acrylic varnish; let it dry for at least 24 hours.

2. For an antique look, apply brown wax shoe polish to the entire surface with a soft cloth. Apply lightly over the white areas and buff with a clean, soft cloth to bring out a glow.

3. Spray several coats of clear varnish on the base and dowel.

4. Glue the dowel to the bird, and attach it to the base.

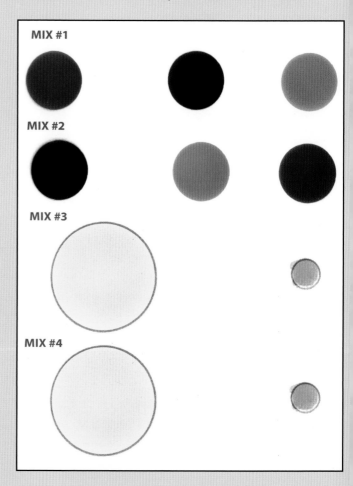

MIX #1

MIX #2

MIX #3

MIX #4

Wood
- Tupelo at least 6" long by 2" by 3"
- ¼"-diameter hardwood dowel
- Scrap wood or tree limb cross section for base

Tools
- Flexible shaft machine or handheld grinder for roughing out, micro motor tool for fine detailing, if necessary

- Medium-grade ball-nosed carbide cutter or bur
- Cylindrical diamond bit
- Round-nosed stump cutter
- Flame-shaped blue stone
- Cylindrical white stone
- $\frac{5}{32}$" or 4mm-diameter brass tubing
- Fine handsaw

Finishing Materials
- Cyanoacrylate (CA) glue
- Cloth-backed sandpaper in a variety of grits
- 12-gauge or 14-gauge copper wire
- Apoxie Sculpt
- Gesso
- Flow medium
- Acrylic paints

Preparing the blank

1 **Cut the block.** Photocopy the side pattern and glue it directly to the wood. Select a piece of wood larger and thicker than the pattern to give the bandsaw blade extra room to maneuver and to keep your fingers a safe distance from the cutting edge.

2 **Mark.** Draw a centerline on both the top and bottom of the cutout.

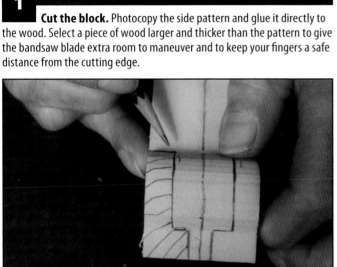

3 **Draw the width of the head and mark off the waste wood.** Keep it blockish at this stage. Leave extra wood on the bill because it is a fragile area and you do not want it too narrow at this stage.

4 **By tilting the cutout, remove the waste wood on the head with the bandsaw.** Use a piece of the wood sawn away from the side profile as a supportive cradle.

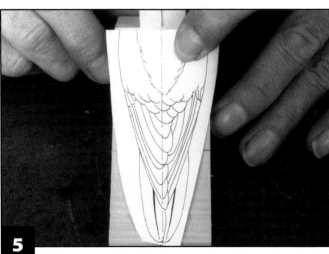

5 **Cut the top profile.** Glue the top profile on the wood and cut it out on the bandsaw. Cradle the cutout with a piece of wood sawn from the side profile.

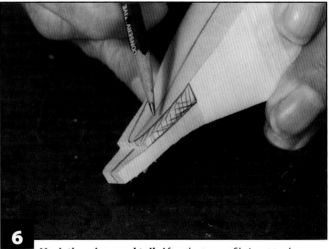

6 **Mark the wings and tail.** After the top profile is cut to shape, mark the thickness of the wings and determine how much wood needs to be removed to separate them from the tail. Make sure that the tail remains straight from front to back, a natural characteristic of all birds.

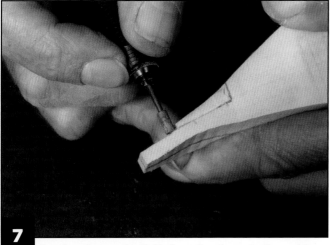

7 **Cut the wings and tail.** Block out the wing and tail separation using a cylindrical diamond bit in a rotary tool. Remove wood using the outline of the wing tip profile as a guide.

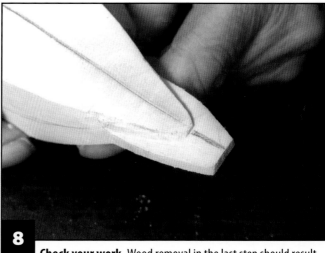

8 **Check your work.** Wood removal in the last step should result in a layered or stepped look. The tip of the wing feathers should be a maximum of ⅛" thick.

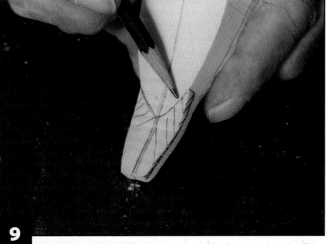

9 **Work the undertail coverts.** Turn the bird over and mark off the undertail covert area. Remove waste wood using the cylindrical diamond bit, leaving about ⅛" to ³⁄₁₆" of wood. If you are aiming for realism, make the tail slightly concave on its underside.

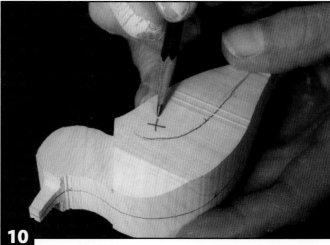

10 **Draw the profile of the wings and mark the widest point of the cutout on both sides.** When rounding the body in the next step, work from the top and bottom centerlines toward those marks.

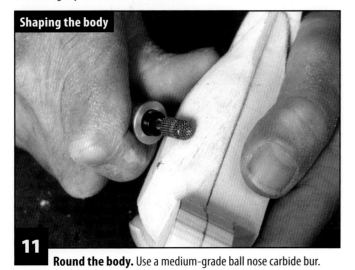

Shaping the body

11 **Round the body.** Use a medium-grade ball nose carbide bur.

12 **Round the breast area.** You want as perfect a circle as you can achieve. Make a cardboard template with a half circle removed from it as a guide if you have trouble visualizing the front profile. Once the breast is rounded, work toward the rear of the bird.

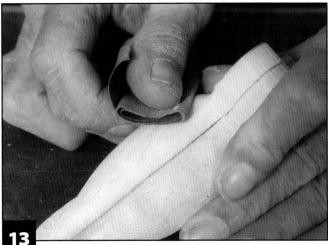

13 **Smooth out the bird.** Burs leave rough grinding marks on the wood. Use the cylindrical diamond bit to smooth the wood as much as possible. Hand sanding also removes coarse marks left by the burs. A cloth-backed sandpaper is a good choice.

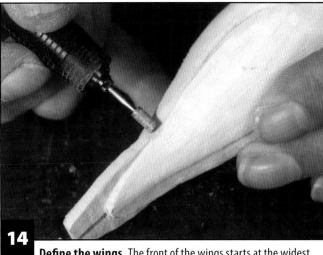

14 **Define the wings.** The front of the wings starts at the widest part of the bird. After penciling in the wing lines, relieve each wing along its bottom edge with the cylindrical diamond bit. The difference in width between a wing and body should be about 1⁄16".

Carving the head

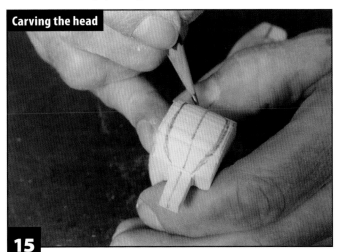

15 **Mark the head.** Pencil in the outline of the head, using the pattern as reference. The eyes are located at the widest part of the head.

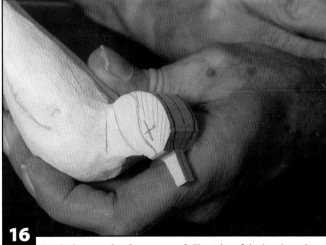

16 **Mark the wood to be removed.** The sides of the head need to be reduced in thickness. However, don't take as much wood away in the cheek areas, which are fuller. Make sure to mark the location of the eyes.

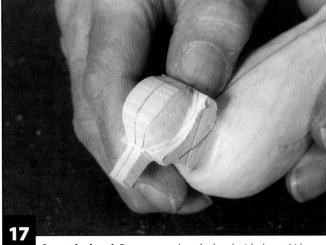

17 **Carve the head.** Remove wood on the head with the carbide cutter used for rounding the body. Do not shape the bill yet.

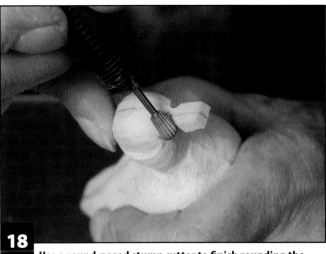

18 **Use a round-nosed stump cutter to finish rounding the head.** The head is egg-shaped, tapered in the front and slightly flat on top. Bring the bill to its final width, making sure to keep it in a straight line with the head. Protect the bill by saturating it with cyanoacrylate (CA) glue.

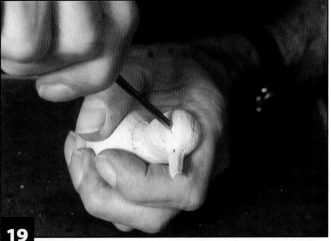

19 **Punch the eyes.** A piece of brass tubing with a wooden handle makes a perfect eye punch. A moderate pressure is required to set the eyes in. If you prefer glass eyes, drill holes and set them in with epoxy putty.

20 **Mark the head for cutting.** The killdeer looks more animated if the head is turned slightly. It is easier to cut the head off and turn it now than it is to carve the head in a turned position. A pencil held at a set height makes for an ideal marking tool. Use a fine handsaw to cut off the head.

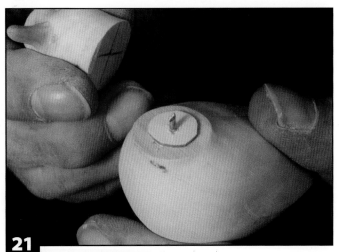

21 **Re-attach the head and body with a short piece of copper wire.** To make up for the saw kerf or thickness, set a piece of cardboard or a thin slice of tupelo on the body to raise the head slightly. Apoxie® Sculpt is a good filler to cover the gap.

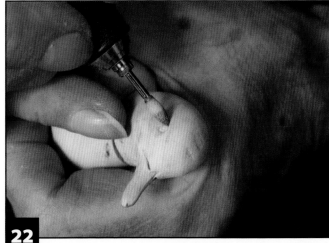

22 **Round the eyes and complete the bill.** Use a flame-shaped blue stone to round the eyes and finish shape the bill.

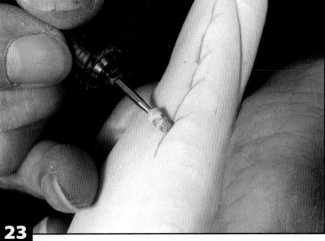

23 **Detail the wing feathers.** For a pleasing finishing touch, delineate the wing feathers using a cylindrical white stone. A burning pen can also be used.

Finishing

24 **Finish.** The final sanding prior to painting is accomplished by using a variety of grits, ranging from 100 to 400. After sanding, select a suitable base and drill holes for the dowel in both the bird and the base. Use a hand drill because it is easier to control the angle of penetration.

Carving Habitat: Twig

By Kenny Vermillion
Photography by Carl Saathoff

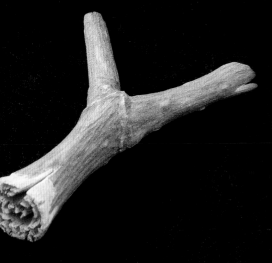

Above: A real twig can be the wrong size for a carving.
Above right: A similar twig used as a habitat element.

Tips on Hand Holding

The twig should always be handheld while carving. Normal breathing causes the hands to independently move uncontrollably. Hold the power carver the same as a pencil, and extend a finger from one hand to touch the other. Now when one hand moves, the other moves with it for coordinated control.

Take a look at the top winners in any bird or wildlife carving competition, and you'll notice many have a common element—a detailed habitat designed to highlight the main subject. You could use actual elements from nature, but they are often the wrong scale and can detract from your overall carving rather than enhance it. By carving your own habitat, you can achieve the specific effect you are striving for and create a professional presentation for your carving.

Examine short sections of a real twig and take note of the interesting details. Figure out how to replicate some of these details on your twig. The variety of colors found in a natural stick make me think of impressionism, and that has influenced how I paint some subjects.

Choose a real, single-forked twig for reference. Carving is a process. First, determine the details you want to incorporate in your own carving and sketch them on the twig. Remove the wood around the details, then break each detail area down into components. When approached in chunks like this, even the most complicated carving becomes achievable. Analyze the colors in the same manner. Gesso the entire carving to prepare the surface for color details. Identify specific areas and the appropriate color. Systematically build cumulative coats of paint to the desired depth of color and finish.

Approach carving and painting as a refining process. From the first cut, it is correcting the shape to conform to the pattern, and from the first coat of gesso it is about correcting the colors. From start to finish, it is a series of corrections.

Roughing out

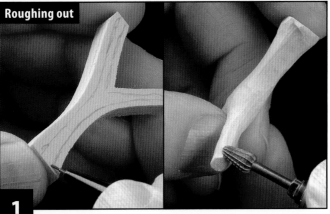

1 Rough out the twig. Divide each side into three equal sections. These lines are important references. Without them, it is easy to remove too much wood, creating a flat or undesired radius. Use a pear-shaped stump cutter to remove the original four corners to the pencil lines to create an octagon. Hold the bit at an oblique angle and carve from the ends toward the center. Round the twig by lightly stroking the bit along it.

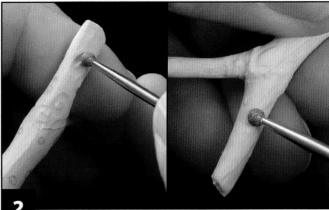

2 Rough out the details. Draw details, such as fissures and buds on the sides. Use a real twig as a reference. Remove wood around each pencil line with a small ball-shaped diamond bur, being careful not to cut too deep. Evenly relieve the wood between the details. Stroke forward because pulling against the rotation creates digs. Use this diamond ball to make the texture and grooves of the bark between and around the details.

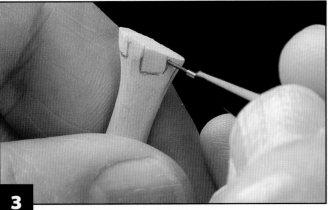

3 Draw the details on the ends of the twig. When a stick is broken, the bark tears unevenly exposing the cambium. The cambium is the layer of tissue below the bark sometimes referred to as the second layer of bark. Sketch some of these tears. When drawing and carving on any project, rather than "grip" the piece, "hold" it. Gripping can cause writer's cramp and, over time, tendonitis.

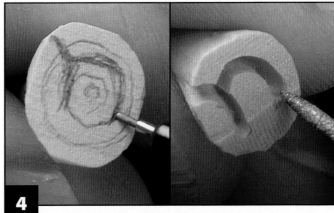

4 Rough in the splits and breaks. Consider the circular growth rings when sketching the splits. Use a tapered-point diamond bur to make the large splits. Increase the depth with each pass. Jamming the bur in will burn the wood. Refer to a real twig to determine cut depth. Use a cylinder-shaped stump cutter to cut the next largest splits. Ease the bit straight into the end of the twig, as a drill bit, and move it sideways to define some splits.

Detailing the ends

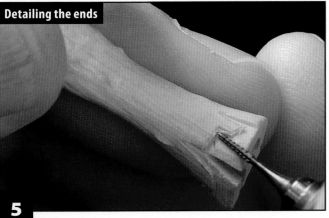

5 Relieve the wood from the perimeter of the ends. Use a tapered stump cutter. There are two layers of bark, and when broken, they sometimes separate and only one is torn off. Notice that these tears may be quite shallow, ragged, and of various lengths.

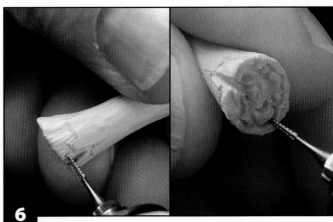

6 Continue detailing the ends. With the tapered stump cutter, etch small splits within the designated areas on the perimeter of each end. Stay with the tapered stump cutter to carve even smaller splits in the twig ends. Continue following the dictates of the growth rings.

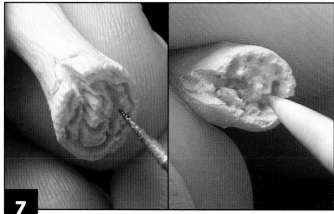

7 **Refine, deepen, and taper the splits.** Use a pointed diamond bur. Use this bit in the same fashion as in Step 4 (like a drill bit). Too much force can break the tip of the bit. This creates even smaller splits and splinters. Lightly buff the splits to remove the fuzz and fragments with the pointed stone. The buffing also rounds the brittle edges to give a time-worn appearance. This stone can also define other features on the twig.

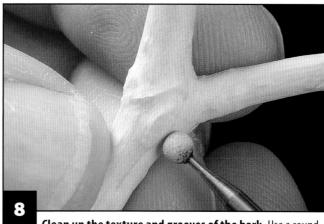

8 **Clean up the texture and grooves of the bark.** Use a round stone to clean up the cuts made by the ball-shaped diamond bit. Refine any detail marks at this time and examine the twig from different angles to spot any areas that need attention. Clean off any remaining pencil marks with an eraser. Stick a straight pin into the end of the twig to aid in clamping for the painting and finishing process.

Painting and finishing

9 **Seal the carving.** Make painting clamps by gluing popsicle sticks to the inside of a clothespin. Notch a dowel and glue it to the outside of the clothespin. I use 5-minute epoxy. A 2 x 4 with accommodating holes serves as a clamp holder. Apply three light coats of interior/exterior lacquer, letting it dry between coats. Allow the lacquer to cure for 12 hours.

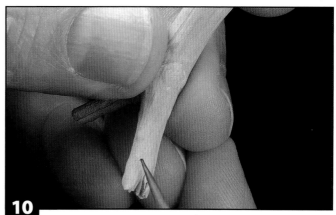

10 **Apply a coat of gesso to the twig.** Using a stiff-bristled brush, mix a couple drops of gesso with water to the consistency of skim milk. Mix thoroughly. Prevent overlap marks by being stingy with the paint and scrubbing the entire surface of the twig. If, after drying, the twig appears evenly coated with no overlaps, one coat is enough. Clean the brush.

11 **Apply a base coat of Payne's gray.** Mix a small amount of Payne's gray with water to the consistency of skim milk. Evenly coat the bark areas of the twig, avoiding the ends and splits. Cover the paint in the well with a wet sponge.

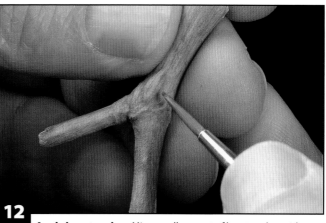

12 **Apply burnt umber.** Mix a small amount of burnt umber with water, to the consistency of skim milk. Paint, keeping the adjacent areas clean. Stir the Payne's gray and repaint. Washes color grooves without filling in details and cover less on high areas, so highlights are automatic. When this coat is dry, re-coat with burnt umber. Repeated washes build the color evenly.

13 **Highlight the details.** Mix a small amount of raw sienna with water to the consistency of skim milk. Paint the exposed cambium layer on the perimeter of the ends. Use the raw sienna wash to paint the small details on the bark. Not only are the details this color, the difference in color further highlights them and makes them more noticeable. Add a couple of drops of water to the raw sienna and paint the splits and splinters on the ends. Also re-coat the cambium layer.

14 **Re-coat the bark.** Stir the Payne's gray, and re-coat all of the bark. Avoid the highlighted details.

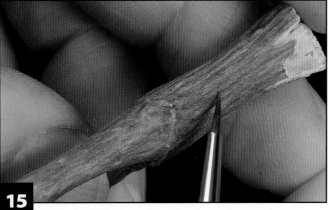

15 **Enhance the darker areas.** After the previous coat has dried, continue to retouch the darker areas with the Payne's gray. After determining how the twig will be placed in the habitat, darken the areas that will be on the bottom, enhancing the natural shading.

Photocopy at 100% or desired size.

Tips on A Carving Work Light

I do all of my work under a 60-watt adjustable arm lamp. Keep the light low and well in front to cast a shadow from the back. This defines contours and depth as opposed to flooding the carving with light, which eliminates shadows.

Materials & Tools

Materials
- ⅜" x 1" x 1½" tupelo or wood of choice
- Acrylic tube paints: raw sienna, burnt umber, Payne's gray
- Gesso
- Interior/exterior spray lacquer
- Palette of choice (I use a plastic egg container)
- Sponges (to place over palette wells to keep paint from drying)
- Three cups of water (one each for mixing paint, initial brush cleaning, and final brush cleaning)
- Paper towels (to clean brush)
- Window cleaner with ammonia (To clean dry acrylic paint)

Tools
- Rotary power carver of choice
- Stump cutters: pear-shaped, cylinder-shaped, tapered-cylinder-shaped
- Stones: Ball-shaped, pointed
- Diamond burs: round, tapered point, pointed
- Stiff-bristled brush, camel hair brush
- Short-bristled nylon brush (to mix paint)
- Old carving knife or painting spatula (to measure paint)
- Eyedropper (to measure water to add to the acrylic paint)

Carving a Dogwood Leaf

Accent your carving with authentic, detailed habitat.

By Kenny Vermillion
Photography by Carl Saathoff

Create a custom habitat by carving leaves from wood. Habitat is a very important aspect of your carving. Over time, the process of creating a carved habitat becomes more natural and comfortable. Carving the habitat adds integrity to the work and credibility to the artist.

To make a pattern of a particular leaf, simply trace around it with a pencil. Real leaves are quite flat. Since we can't carve wood comparably as thin, ours look too bulky. Exaggerate the arcs and curls in the carved leaf to fool the eye; this is a sculpting technique employed since ancient times.

Every leaf I carve is from a new drawing. I sketch a new outline and saw it from a piece of tupelo at least one-fourth as thick as it is long. This thickness permits spontaneous shaping. The leaf can be curled up, down, or sideways; the center vein can be deep or shallow; and the perimeters can be flipped or bent in any direction. The resulting top shape dictates the bottom shape. When the extra wood is carved from the bottom it can be left thicker in the center for strength, but the extra thickness isn't noticeable because of the exaggerated contours.

The leaf is always handheld while carving. Normal breathing causes the hands to move independently from one another. Hold the power carver the same as a pencil and extend a finger from one hand to touch the other. Now both hands will move together in a coordinated motion.

Roughing out the leaves and veins

1 **Draw the center vein.** Pull a large, flame-shaped diamond bit at a 45° angle from each end toward the center. Make several passes until the depth of the vein is ⅛" deep at the stem and ⅛" from the bottom of the blank at the tip. The depth is constant from the stem to the center of the leaf. From the center, it arcs down to the tip. Do not remove too much wood at one time. This will overload the diamond bit and may damage the power carver.

2 **Rough shape the top of the leaf.** Use the same bit to remove the wood between the center vein and the outside edge. The leaf bulges slightly from the center vein to the outside edge. Carve from the center out, holding the carver at an angle. If you run the carver perpendicular to the edge, it may roll over the edge and ruin the leaf. Work on one side first, then carve the opposite side. The leaf should taper down at the tip.

3 **Add in the other veins.** Draw the veins with a pencil. Then, trace along these lines with the tip of a tapered stone to create a furrow along the length of the vein. These furrows set the stage for the use of a larger bit later. Power carvers pull in the direction they rotate, so it is easier to start with a smaller, less aggressive bit.

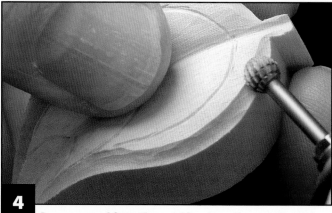

4 **Remove wood from the outside edges.** Use a small, round stump cutter to remove approximately ¹⁄₁₆" from the stem. Create a taper along the edge from the stem down to the tip. Stroke with the rotation of the bit for more control. This is an aggressive bit, so use caution and don't allow the bit to roll over the edge of the leaf and create a divot.

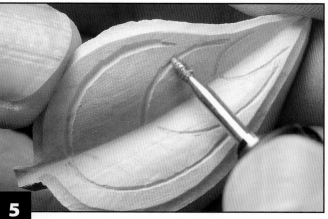

5 **Deepen the side veins on the top of the leaf.** Use a small, flame-shaped diamond bit to remove wood, making the side veins about ¹⁄₃₂" deep. The furrows you made in Step 3 make it easier to control this more aggressive bit. Do not extend the veins the whole way to the edge or overcarve into the center vein.

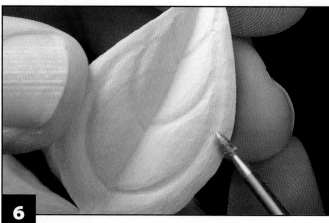

6 **Contour the leaf between the veins.** Use a small, flame-shaped diamond bit to create a gentle arc between the veins. Maintain the V shape at the bottom of the veins. Use the same bit to shape the contours between the veins and perimeter. The leaf arcs out from the veins and sweeps out to the edge of the leaf.

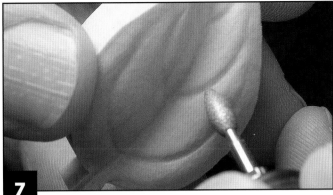

7 **Smooth and refine the top of the leaf.** Set the power carver at a high rpm. Use a reduced-grit, bonded ruby bit (see reducing a bonded ruby bit at right). This bit cuts smoothly, but does not destroy details like sandpaper. Slowly pull the bit from the center toward the edge. Use the side of the tip to define the veins. Stroke diagonally across the grain to smooth each section between the veins.

Reducing a bonded ruby bit

Usually the ruby grit is inconsistent and coarse, but it can be reduced on a diamond strop. To reduce the grit, run the bit at a high speed and carefully brush it across a diamond strop. Rubies are softer than diamonds, so the diamond will reduce the grit of the ruby. It is very important to use the same strokes from the hilt to the point. Frequently run the side of the bit on a piece of scrap wood to test for spikes and inconsistencies. Use caution; removing all of the grit will render the ruby bit useless. The general shape of this bit cannot be altered, because it is metal.

Carving the underside

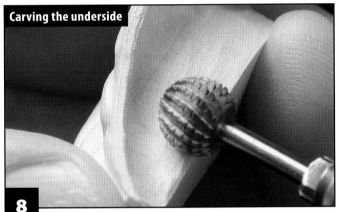

8 **Rough out the bottom of the leaf.** Guide a large, round stump cutter just under the leaf. Keep the angle and direction of the rotation away from the leaf top and carve about 1/16" deep. Keep the leaf at least 1/32" thick. The contours of the top of the leaf dictate the shape of the bottom. Close in on the center from each side. Leave the leaf thicker in the center.

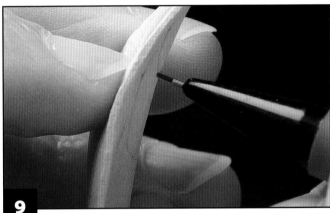

9 **Smooth the bottom and sketch the veins.** Switch between a large, round stump cutter and a large, flame-shaped diamond bit to smooth the bottom. Then, mark the location of the veins. Hold the leaf vertically. Point to the location where the side veins meet the center vein with your fingernail and transfer the position to the bottom of the leaf with a pencil.

10 **Shape the underside.** Relieve the wood from around the veins with a small, round stump cutter. While the veins are represented by V-cuts on the top, they are represented by raised lines on the bottom. Reduce the thickness of the edges and create a transition to the thicker wood in the center. Hold the same bit parallel to the edges, and be careful not to run over the end.

11 **Detail the veins.** Use a bullet-nosed stone to outline the veins and smooth the relieved areas between them. Then, smooth the underside of the outer edge. The stone smooths the area between the veins and prepares the carving for the final painting. I prefer the bullet-nosed stone because the shape allows me to smooth between the raised veins without damaging them.

Gauging wood thickness

Frequently hold the leaf to the edge of a 60-watt lamp. A surprising amount of light will pass through a thick piece of tupelo or basswood. Compare the light near the edge to the light in the center. If an area appears too thin, mark it with a pencil.

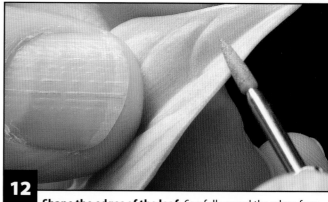

12 **Shape the edges of the leaf.** Carefully round the edges from both the top and bottom with the side of a pointed stone. The rounded edge will appear thinner and will not chip as easily as a thin, square edge. Use the same stone to refine and shape the stem. View the leaf from different angles to spot any areas that need further refining.

Painting and finishing

13 **Seal the carving.** Stick a small straight pin into the stem. I hold the pin in a shop-made clamp. To make the clamp, use five-minute epoxy to adhere a half of a craft stick to the inside of both sides of a clothespin. Glue the clothespin to a dowel and insert the dowel in a hole drilled in a piece of scrap wood. Apply three or four light coats of lacquer. Allow the lacquer to set for 12 hours.

14 **Apply a coat of gesso.** Gesso provides an opaque primer base and better paint adherence. Always mix with a stiff-bristled brush and apply with a camel hair brush. Mix a couple drops with water to the consistency of milk. Mix thoroughly to dissolve. Pick up a small amount on the very tip of the brush and wipe one side against the well. Paint from the center vein out, one section at a time, with as few strokes as possible. Recoat as needed. Make sure the gesso is dry between coats.

15 **Apply the yellow base coat.** Use an old knife to scrape a small amount of paint from the tube. Wipe the paint against the side of the palette well and use an eyedropper to add water. Dip the stiff-bristled brush in water and mix up the paint wash. Add water as needed to create a skim milk consistency. Paint the front, back, and stem of the leaf using a camel hair brush. Apply a second coat after the first coat has thoroughly dried.

16 **Highlight the veins.** Mix two parts brilliant yellow and one part Hooker's green with water to the consistency of skim milk. Touch the tip of a brush to the paint and lightly wipe one side on the well. Touch the point to the outside edge next to the center vein. Hold the brush slightly on its side with the ferrule towards the section's vein and stroke along the outside perimeter. Repeat on the other side. The perimeters of each section should be green and the centers yellow.

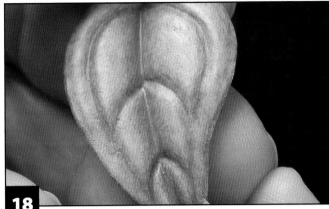

17 **Add additional coats of the paint mixture.** Blending acrylic paints with only one coat is very difficult. More pleasing results are achieved by overlapping multiple thin coats. Each coat must be dry before applying the next. Thin paint is key. Be stingy with the paint. Each coat overlaps the others to cover a slightly broader area and provides a pleasing shade to the leaf.

18 **Add a homogenizing wash.** Add one part raw sienna to the existing paint mixture. Paint the top of the leaf with the wash to tie all of the colors together. Paint the underside of the leaf with the same mixture. The underside of the leaf is much lighter than the top. Because it is a lighter color, it does not require as much paint. Be careful not to apply too much paint.

19 **Paint the veins on the underside of the leaf.** Thin brilliant yellow with water to the consistency of whole milk. Coat the veins with the wash. Then, paint the top and bottom of the leaf with raw sienna thinned to the consistency of skim milk. Go back and re-paint the veins with the brilliant yellow. Add a final wash of raw sienna to the top of the leaf.

Materials & Tools

Materials
- ½" x 1¼" x 2" tupelo or wood of choice
- Acrylic tube paints: brilliant yellow, Hooker's green, and raw sienna
- Gesso
- Bottle of window cleaner with ammonia (to further clean acrylic paint off brushes)

Tools
- Rotary power carver of choice
- Stones: bullet nose, tapered, and pointed
- Large, flame-shaped ruby bit with reduced grit
- Stump cutters: small round and large round
- Diamond bits: small flame and large flame

- Painting clamps (clothespins glued to dowels)
- Clamp holder (a short 2 x 4 with holes for the dowels)
- 3 cups of water (for mixing paint, and for brush cleaning)
- Paper towels (to wipe brushes)
- Eyedropper (to dispense water)
- Knife or plastic spatula (to measure paint)
- Short-bristled nylon brush (to mix paint)
- Pointed camel hair brush (to apply paint)
- Paint palette (I use plastic egg trays because they have deep wells)
- Wet sponges (to place over paint to prevent it from drying)
- Coffee can lid (to hold the wet sponges when not in use)

Photocopy at 100% or desired size.

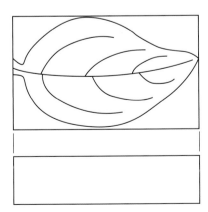

Carving Habitat: Mushroom

by Kenny Vermillion
photography by Carl Saathoff

This is a good project to expand and develop your power carving and painting techniques. Perceived mistakes can be enhanced and incorporated into the design. Mushrooms come in an interesting variety of shapes and sizes. With a range of suitable colors, they make intriguing primary subjects or supporting elements of habitat.

Most power carvers prefer tupelo, but there are other types of wood that will work. Orient the grain vertically from top to bottom for both the stem and the cap. After cutting out the blank, sand the bottom of the stem flat with 120-grit sandpaper. Place the sandpaper flat on a table, and pull the bottom of the stem evenly across the paper.

When working on this project, hold the blank in your hand. Normal breathing causes the hands to move independently from each other. Increase stability by extending one finger to the other hand, in effect anchoring the hands together. Now when one hand moves, the other moves with it, enabling coordinated control.

Increase control by establishing a contact point between both hands causing them to move in tandem.

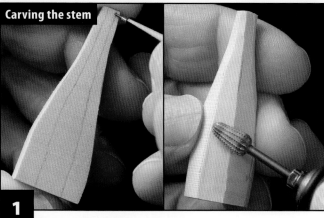

1 Remove the corners of the stem. Divide the length of all four sides into three equal sections with a pencil. Use a pear-shaped stump cutter to remove the corners back to these lines, creating an octagon-shaped stem. Hold the cutter at an oblique angle, and carve from the ends toward the center.

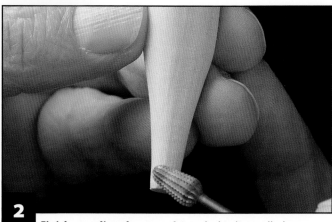

2 Finish rounding the stem. Orient the bit diagonally, keep it flat, and lightly stroke forward with the rotation of the bit. This is an opportunity to further develop control. Proceeding around the stem, each stroke should further smooth the surface.

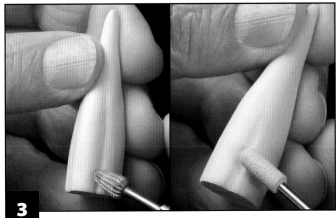

3 **Add grooves to the sides of the stem.** Lightly sketch three grooves of varying lengths, unevenly spaced around the stem, with the longest slightly more than half the stem. Use a pear-shaped stump cutter to carve them to different depths and widths. Round the side of each groove. Smooth the entire stem with a round-nosed cylinder stone.

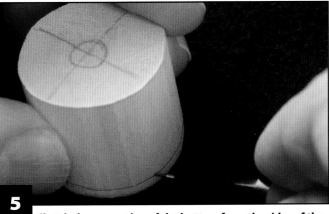

5 **Sketch the separation of the bottom from the sides of the mushroom.** Draw a line ¹⁄₁₆" up from the bottom of the cap around the circumference of the blank. Hold the eraser end of a pencil on the table while holding the point against the blank. To draw an even line, do not move the pencil; instead, rotate the blank against the pencil.

7 **Round the bottom of the cap.** Work from approximately ¹⁄₈" inside the center hole to the larger circle line with a pear-shaped stump cutter. Relieve the wood from the line made in Step 5 toward the center hole, rounding the area to the larger circle line. Because you are working with the end grain, stroke the bit at oblique angles to the grain, to avoid digging out the soft grain.

Carving the cap

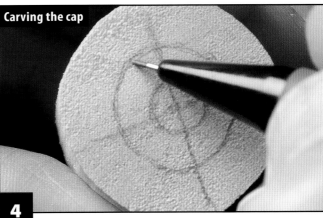

4 **Mark the layout lines on the cap.** Divide the top and bottom of the cap into four sections to find the center and then draw a small reference circle around the center. On the bottom, draw a larger circle, half the distance from the center to the edge. The smaller circle is where the stem will fit, and the larger circle is the centerline for rounding the bottom of the cap.

6 **Carve the hole for the stem.** Use a taper-point diamond bit. Make short, vertical strokes straight into the center, and then move the bit in small circles to make the hole bigger than the bit. This method avoids damage to the tools. After you've reached a depth of ³⁄₈", pull the bit to the sides of the first circle. Use the stem to judge the diameter. You want a snug fit.

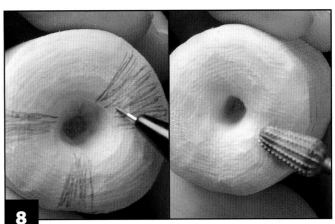

8 **Add some uneven areas to the bottom.** Sketch three random areas of various widths to add a softer appearance to the rounded bottom. Using the same stump cutter, remove the wood within these areas, guided by the previously established rounding. More wood is removed as you move from the center to the outside. The result should be a smooth, flowing contour.

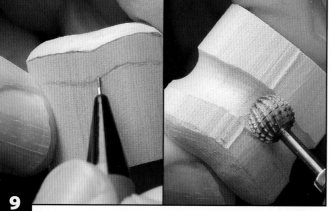

9 **Rough out the cap.** Draw a line following the bottom contour on the outside perimeter of the cap. Draw a second contour line about 3/16" above the first line representing the bulkiness of the cap. Guide a large round stump cutter across the grain to remove wood above the second line.

10 **Continue removing wood from the cap.** Use a round stump cutter to carve channels from the top to the channel carved in Step 9. Then, remove the wood between channels. Hold the bit perpendicular to the circle on the top and reduce the tip to the diameter of the circle. Create a smooth taper from the tip down.

Detailing the cap

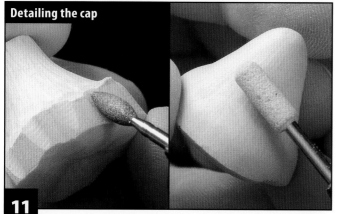

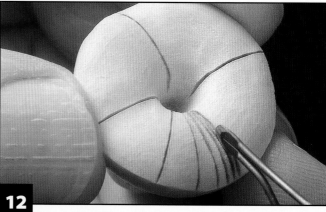

11 **Detail the tip and base.** Use a large flame-shaped diamond bit to angle the side into the base of the cap. Maintain a sharp juncture where the base and underside meet. Remove 1/16" of wood from the top of the base to angle the side toward the peak. Round the peak of the cap. Round the edge at the top of the base portion, creating a slightly concave shape from the base to the tip. Use a cylinder stone to smooth the entire cap.

12 **Burn in the gills on the bottom of the cap.** Divide the underside into quarters. Make a controlled, shallow burn along the lines with a rounded (J) tip at a low temperature. Push the tip from the outside edge toward the center; pulling the tip obscures your view. Do not burn the angled edge. Divide these sections into halves. The gills appear softer if they are close together. Randomly burn a few of the gills up into the angled edge to represent splits.

Painting and finishing

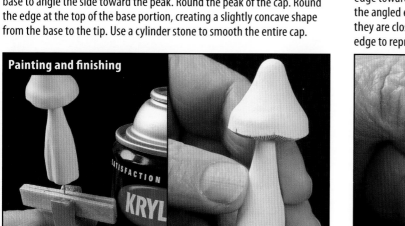

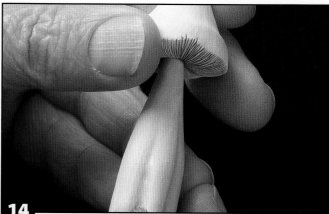

13 **Prepare for painting.** Apply five-minute epoxy in the hole of the cap. Insert the stem and let this cure. Spray three or four light coats of lacquer. Allow to cure for 12 hours. Mix a couple drops of white gesso with water to the consistency of milk. Sparingly scrub the entire surface, except for the bottom of the stem. Use a camel hair brush and apply a second coat if needed.

14 **Paint the stem.** Use an old knife to scrape a small amount of paint from the end of the tube. Mix a small amount of raw sienna with water to the consistency of skim milk. Paint the gills and the stem, and let it dry. Cover the paint in the palette with a damp sponge. When the paint is dry, repaint the gills, the top 1/2" of the stem under the cap, and the channels in the lower half of the stem.

15 **Add shadows to the gills and upper stem.** Apply another coat of paint to the gills and the stem immediately under the cap. Because of natural lighting, this area would be more shaded than the channels in the bottom of the stem. For a smoother blending of paint, overlap or underlap the first coat when repainting the top part of the stem.

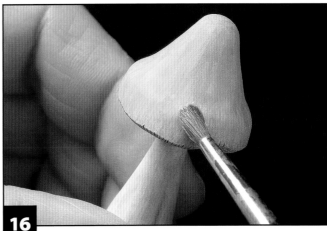

16 **Paint the top of the cap.** Mix a small amount of yellow oxide with water to the consistency of whole milk. Apply the first coat to the top of the cap. This coat must be dry before applying the second. Apply the second coat of yellow oxide to the top of the cap. After it is dry, check it for even coverage to determine if another coat is needed.

Stippling

17 **Stipple paint the tip of the cap.** Mix a small amount of burnt sienna with water to the consistency of milk. Touch the tip of the brush to the paint and lightly wipe one side of the brush. Dab the brush onto a paper towel. Lightly tap the paintbrush from the peak of the cap to two-thirds of the way down the sides. The brush gradually runs out of paint, so the coat gradually gets thinner. When dry, repeat, but only go one-half way down. After it has dried, retouch as needed to ensure the peak is fully covered and there is a gradual blend into the yellow oxide.

Materials & Tools

Materials

- 1" x 1" x 1" tupelo or wood of choice (cap)
- ⅝" x ⅝" x 2" tupelo or wood of choice (stem)
- Lacquer spray
- Acrylic tube paints: yellow oxide, raw sienna, burnt sienna
- Gesso
- Five-minute epoxy
- Palette of choice
- Sponges (to place over palette wells to keep paint from drying)
- 3 cups of water (for mixing paint, and for brush cleaning)
- Paper towels (to clean brushes)
- Window cleaner with ammonia (solvent for acrylic paint)

Tools

- Carving burs: taper-point and large flame-shaped diamond burs, round-nosed cylinder stone, pear-shaped and large round stump cutters
- Woodburner and rounded tip burning pen
- Pointed camel hair brush (to apply paint)
- Short-bristled nylon brush (to mix paint)
- Old carving knife or painting spatula (to measure paint)
- Eyedropper (to measure water)
- Clothespin clamp

Photocopy at 100% or desired size.

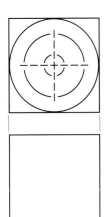

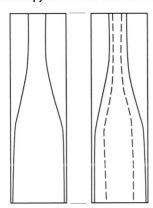

Mushroom cap
1" x 1" x 1"

Mushroom stem
2" x ⅝" x ⅝"

Walking Stick Wizard

By Frank Russell

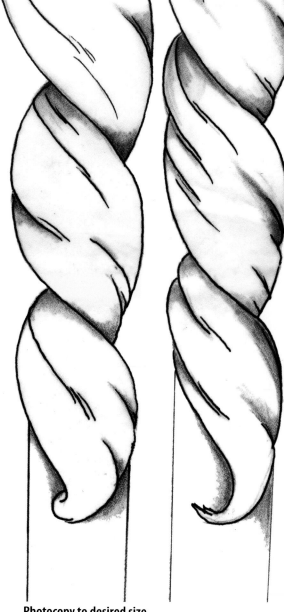

Photocopy to desired size

Materials & Tools

Materials:
- Straight limb, size of choice
- Glue stick
- Natural staining oil
- Flat or matte lacquer or exterior-grade polyurethane
- Raw umber and Mars black acrylic paints (for antiquing wash) (optional)
- Metal or rubber cane tip (optional)

Tools:
- Band saw or scroll saw
- Small and medium flame-shaped carbide burs
- Small and medium flame-shaped ruby carver
- Medium bud-shaped ruby carver
- Small ball-shaped diamond bit
- Small flame-shaped diamond bit
- Medium inverted cone-shaped safe end diamond bit and small sharp inverted cone-shaped diamond bit
- Defuzzing mandrel or rotary bristle brush
- Small cylinder-shaped stone bit

A good straight limb from a tree can be used after removing the bark and seasoning, but for the purpose of this book, the stick part was turned on a lathe, and a carving block was left on top. Of course, the length, size, and shape of the block will depend on what you plan to carve on top of the walking stick.

I was certainly glad to see the end of the beard—I didn't think I'd ever care to texture hair again after I completed this project. I still haven't given the man a price who wants one with a little bigger head and a beard that winds all the way to the bottom!

Cutting the blank

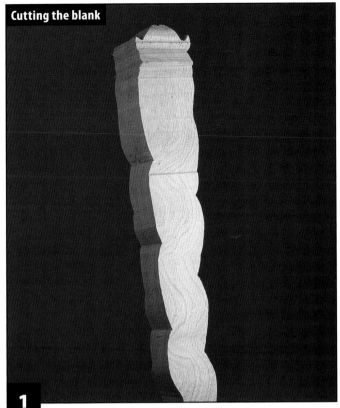

1 **Cut the blank two ways on the bandsaw.** I copy my drawings to the desired size on a photocopier, and then I use a glue stick to glue them directly to the stock while I saw along the drawn lines.

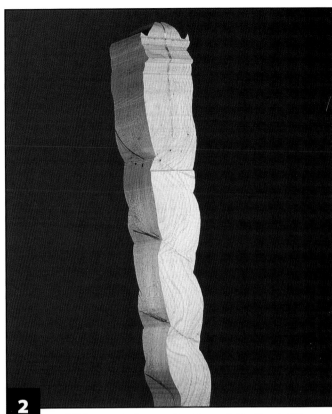

2 **Establish a vertical centerline through the front of the face area.** Draw any wasting or rough shaping lines over the entire blank.

3 **Rough shape entire carving.** Use a small and medium flame-shaped carbide bur.

4 **Shape contours of the face—eye mounds, nose, cheeks, and forehead.** Finish shape head hair and entire beard. Use medium flame-shaped and bud-shaped ruby carvers.

Detailing the face

5   **Detail the face—eyes, nose, cheeks, forehead, and wrinkles.** Use the small flame-shaped ruby carver and small ball-shaped diamond bit for the nostril holes.

6   **Texture the hair over entire piece.** Use the medium inverted cone-shaped safe end diamond bit for the beard and hair, the small sharp inverted cone-shaped diamond bit where the beard and mustache meet the face, the small cylinder-shaped stone for the eyebrows, and the small flame-shaped diamond bit to clean up detail. Clean and defuzz with a defuzzing mandrel or rotary bristle brush.

Finishing Schedule

7   **Finish.** Touch up any details, clean with a rotary brush or defuzzer, and then enhance the grain with a natural staining oil. Allow to dry thoroughly. Finish with flat or matte lacquer or exterior-grade polyurethane. This project is for outdoor use and will undoubtedly see many miles.

8   **Add an antiquing wash.** If greater depth is desired, wash raw umber/Mars black over the stick. This leaves residue in the depressions and enhances the carved detail. Seal the carving with two coats of exterior-grade finish. Finish the bottom with a metal cane stud and a rubber crutch tip.

Maple Leaf Pin

By Kenny Vermillion
photography by Carl Saathoff

Allison models the pin with the matching earrings.

This delightful fall accent can be worn alone or paired with the leaf earrings on page 79. The pin uses the same techniques used to create the earrings, but is more advanced due to the multiple layers.

A pattern for the pin is offered below. Keep in mind that a pattern is to be interpreted—not followed as a blueprint. Feel free to alter the pattern, experiment with different techniques or change the colors. These minor changes personalize your work and build confidence.

I use tupelo, but you can use the wood and tools of your choice. I show you what I use and how I use it, but if you have a tool that will work instead, that is great. As you become more dexterous, your work will become more refined.

All of my subjects are carved with the same general philosophy:

- I believe in good work habits. There are no practice pieces.

- Know your subject—thoroughly.

- Don't overwhelm yourself. You must visualize every step from start to finish.

- Carving and painting is a series of corrections. Correct every mistake as soon as you see it.

- Keep your work neat from start to finish.

- Develop a light touch. Finesse achieves more pleasing results than force.

- Critique and analysis—positive and continuous.

- Desire supersedes patience. Time is insignificant.

All of that sounds rather stern, but that doesn't mean we don't have fun. Of what good can it be if it isn't enjoyable? Developing my power carving and painting skills has been extremely gratifying. I hope you find it equally so.

Photocopy at 100%

Cutting the layers

1 **Cut out the blank.** Transfer the pattern to stock with flat grain running parallel to the center veins. Cut the blank and sand the back with 220-grit sandpaper. Lightly draw the pattern lines with a pencil. Only draw the veins on the top leaf. The piece should be handheld while carving. Normal breathing causes the hands to move independently from each other. Hold the power carver like a pencil, and extend a finger from one hand to touch the other so your hands move in unison.

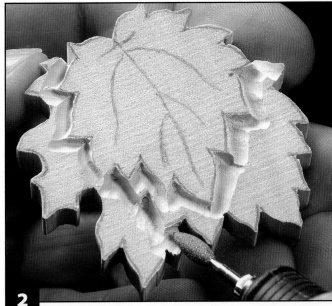

2 **Outline the leaves.** Use a large, flame-shaped diamond bit to follow the pencil lines. Outline the top and center leaves. Do not carve the veins at this time. Create shallow furrows by lightly pulling the bit. Rotary bits pull to one side, and they are easier to control with lighter pressure. Once the furrow is established, the bit is easier to control. Deepen the furrows to approximately ¼ the thickness of the blank, creating a 90° side.

3 **Create three separate leaves.** Reduce the thickness of the second and third leaves using the side of a cylinder stump cutter. This bit is aggressive, so use caution. These levels should come straight out from the furrows to create a layer for each leaf. Lightly stroke with the rotation of the bit, avoiding the outer edges of the middle and top leaves. Keep the bit flat and rotate the carving as needed to avoid running the cutter over the edges. Keep your fingers out of the path of the cutter.

4 **Refine the leaves.** The cylinder shape is inappropriate for close work between the leaves. Use the tip of a large flame-shaped diamond bit to refine the ragged sides between the leaves. The point of this bit fits into the serrated perimeter of the leaves. Maintain the 90° sides between the leaves. Use the same bit to smooth the rough surface left by the stump cutter. The goal is to have flat planes. Orient the bit diagonally, and stroke from the outside edge toward the center to protect the outside edges.

Defining the veins

5 **Carve in the basic veins.** Lightly draw curved veins on the second and third leaves, using the pattern as a guide. The side veins originate from the center vein and extend to the leaf points. Use a small flame-shaped diamond bit to start the veins. Pull the point to create shallow furrows from the centers toward the edges. Stop before reaching the edge, because the bit hides the leaf point from view. Rotate the leaf and carve from the outside edges toward the center, connecting the furrows.

6 **Deepen and contour the veins.** Use the side of the diamond bit's point. The center vein of the top leaf is higher in the center and lower at the base. It sweeps down from the center and back up at the tip. The two short veins near the tip and the two long veins start at the center vein and go up slightly. The two short veins at the base bow up. The center vein of the middle leaf arcs down at the tip. The succeeding veins on both sides curve up. On the bottom leaf, the center vein arcs down at the tip. The short veins closest to the tip bow up. The next two veins arc down. The last vein, near the base, bows up.

7 **Contour the leaves between the veins.** Using the side of the tip of the same diamond bit, follow the contour of the veins, and relieve the wood from both sides of the veins. The areas between the veins sweep and flow smoothly. The arcs and bows at the points of the veins direct the shape variation of the leaf edges. While contouring the leaf tops, maintain the 90° sides where the leaves overlap. Notice how the areas between the veins blend. Do not leave any flat spots.

8 **Refine and smooth the veins.** I favor modified ruby bits over sandpaper. Sandpaper flattens the details. Reduce the grit of a ruby bit by brushing it lightly against a diamond hone at a high rpm. Test the bit on a piece of scrap for spikes and inconsistencies. Do not remove all the grit! Pull the modified ruby bit slowly from the center toward the edge at a high rpm. Use the side of the tip to define the veins. Smooth each section between the veins. Stroking diagonally across the grain will smooth it evenly.

Intermediate

Attaching the pin

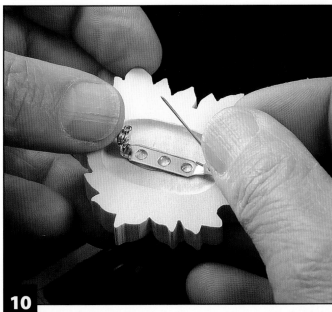

9 **Hollow out the recess for the pin.** Transfer the pattern to the back of the carving. Use an egg-shaped stump cutter to relieve the area to accommodate the pin. Stay inside the pencil line. Carve a series of diagonal lines across the area $\frac{1}{16}$" deep. Clean out the recess, using slow, forward strokes for consistent depth. A flat bottom is important for the pin to sit squarely. Smooth the relieved area with an aluminum oxide stone. The stone I use was originally ball shaped, modified to a slight bullet shape on the diamond strop. The side of the bullet shape smooths more evenly than a ball.

10 **Epoxy the pin in the recess.** I use 5-minute epoxy. Mix the epoxy with a toothpick. Squeeze out small, equal amounts of epoxy and hardener, and mix thoroughly with a toothpick. There is a short working time with 5-minute epoxy. If it strings from the toothpick when you pick it up, the epoxy has already started to set up. It will not adhere well and should not be used. Neatly apply the glue to the underside of the pin, avoiding the hinge and lock. Orient the pin with the hinge to the right. Moderately press the pin into position. Let the epoxy harden for at least 5 minutes.

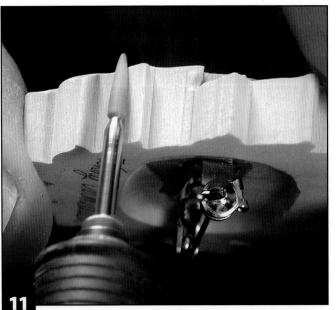

11 **Enhance the texture of the edges.** Use the side of a reduced-diameter ruby stone at a high rpm to lightly soften the saw marks. Hold the stone parallel to the saw marks, and stroke carefully to maintain them evenly up and down the sides. To reduce the diameter of the ruby stone, run it against a diamond strop or dressing stone at a moderate rpm. Do not remove the stone all the way to the shaft; use the bonding agent and metal shaft as a visual guide. Proceed carefully; friction can overheat the stone and degrade the integrity of the bonding agent.

12 **Texture the edges of the middle and bottom leaves.** Use a reduced-diameter ruby stone to refine the 90° sides between the overlapped leaves. Carefully follow the contour of the middle and bottom leaf. Replicate the vertical saw marks onto the overlapping sides. Wooden 90° edges chip and break. Slightly round the edges on both the top and bottom of the sides completely around each leaf. Use the side of the tip of the ruby stone at a moderate rpm.

13 **Seal the pin.** Sign the back of the pin with pencil before sealing the carving. I create small clamps by gluing popsicle sticks to clothespins and gluing the clothespins to dowels. Drill holes matching the dowel size in a scrap piece of wood so you can insert the clamp to allow the piece to dry. Clamp the pin hardware between the popsicle sticks and apply three to four light coats of interior/exterior lacquer spray. Spray the entire pin, front, back, and sides. This prevents the grain from rising when painting with washes. Allow the lacquer to dry for at least 12 hours, then peel the lacquer from the pin hardware.

14 **Apply a base coat of gesso.** Using a stiff-bristled brush, mix a couple drops of white gesso with water to the consistency of milk. Mix thoroughly to ensure all particles are dissolved. Wet a camel hair brush with clean water and put a small amount of gesso on the very tip. Wipe one side of it on the edge of the palette well. Paint from the center vein out, one section at a time, with as few strokes as possible. The sides and the back of the leaves do not require gesso, only the tops. Half of the top leaf shows two coats, and the other half has one coat. Notice the even coverage. Subsequent coats are required if coverage is uneven.

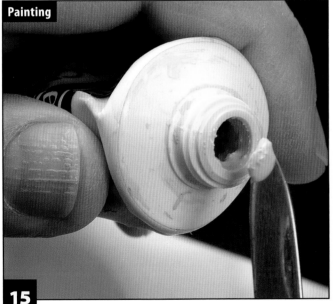

Painting

15 **Mix a wash of brilliant yellow paint.** I use an old knife to scrape a small amount of paint from the end of the tube. With practice, measurements can be consistently made this way. Wipe the measured portion of the paint into the side of a well on your palette and use an eyedropper to add a couple drops of water. Use a stiff-bristled brush, first dipped in water, to mix the paint. Add water as needed to get the consistency of skim milk.

16 **Base coat the leaves.** Use a camel hair brush. Always wet your brush with clean water before picking up any paint. This photo shows the leaves with one coat. Two coats are required. Cover the paint in the palette with a wet sponge while the first coat is drying. Blending acrylic paints with only one coat is very difficult. More pleasing results are achieved with multiple, thin coats that overlap or underlap. Each coat must be dry before applying the next. Thin paint is key. Be stingy with the paint.

17 **Paint the top leaf.** Add a touch of cadmium red light to the yellow paint mix to get a creamy orange color. Touch the tip of the brush to the paint, and lightly wipe one side on the well to make sure the brush is not overloaded. Touch the brush's point to the outside edge next to the center vein; hold the brush slightly on its side with the ferrule angled toward the section's vein. Stroke along the outside perimeter to the end of the side vein. Repeat on the other side of the section, the full length of the vein, to meet the outside stroke. The perimeters of each section should be orange and the centers should be yellow. Paint each remaining section of the leaf in the same manner.

18 **Apply a second coat.** After the first coat has thoroughly dried, repeat the process on the top leaf. The second coat will overlap the first and cover a slightly broader area. Use the same mixture to add color to the middle leaf. Apply the paint in the same manner, but only on the veins and as a shadow around the perimeter where the top leaf meets the surface of the middle leaf. Apply a second coat to the middle leaf after the first has dried. Stir the paint frequently because the pigments are heavier than water and settle to the bottom.

19 **Apply a homogenizing wash.** Increase the orange color volume by one-third with water, and stir it well. Apply this wash to the entire surface of the first and second leaves. This wash ties the colors together. One coat should be enough. Save this color for Step 22. Allow sufficient time for the wash to dry thoroughly. The middle leaf is now ready for the red color.

Stippling

20 **Stipple a coat of cadmium red medium paint over the middle leaf.** Stippling is lightly tapping and dabbing. In a clean well, mix the paint with water to the consistency of skim milk. Touch the tip of the brush to the paint, and dab the brush onto a paper towel to to remove any excess paint. Start on the points of the leaf, and lightly stipple toward the base. Avoid the veins and the area around the perimeter of the top leaf. Allow the paint to dry thoroughly. Two to four coats will be required. The outside of the leaf and the area between the veins should be red and gradually blend into the orange.

21 **Paint the veins on the bottom leaf.** Mix eight parts yellow and one part Hookers green with water to the consistency of skim milk. Hookers green is a very intense color and it is difficult to gauge how much to mix. Adjustments may be made to suit individual taste. Use the same techniques you used on the top leaf to wet blend the green into the veins of the bottom leaf. Allow the first coat to dry and apply a second coat. After the second coat has dried, a touch up coat may need to be stippled on. Stippling is an effective way to darken the center of the veins and the perimeter of the overlaying leaf.

22 **Prepare a final wash for the green leaf.** Increase the volume of the green paint by one-third with water and add a touch of the orange from Step 19. Because green is such an intense color, the orange is added to tone it down. One coat should be enough, but more can be applied, or a wash of the orange mixture can be added. Mixing paint is imprecise; adjustments are just part of the process.

Finishing

23 **Paint the edges of the leaves.** In a new well, mix burnt sienna, a very small amount of acra violet, and a couple drops of water to a consistency of thick cream. Using light vertical strokes (follow the saw marks), paint the sides with this color all the way around each leaf. Too much pressure on the brush will squeeze paint onto the top and bottom of the leaf. Mix gloss medium and varnish with water to the consistency of milk. Put one coat on the top, being careful not to get it on the sides. This establishes two finishes for visual interest.

Materials & Tools

Materials:
- ⅜" x 2" x 2" tupelo
- Pin back of choice
- 5-minute epoxy
- Toothpick (to mix epoxy)
- Wet sponge (to keep paint in palette from drying out)
- Window cleaner with ammonia (to clean brushes)
- Palette
- White gesso
- Acrylic tube paints: brilliant yellow, cadmium red light, cadmium red medium, Hookers green, burnt sienna, acra violet

Tools:
- Power carver of choice
- Mechanical pencil with .5mm HB lead
- Sandpaper, 220 grit
- Large, flame-shaped diamond bur
- Cylinder stump cutter
- Small, flame-shaped diamond bur
- Reduced-grit, bonded ruby bur
- Fine-grit diamond hone
- Egg-shaped stump cutter
- Ball-shaped aluminum oxide stone
- Reduced-diameter ruby stone
- Old carving knife (to measure paint)
- Paintbrushes of choice (at least one stiff-bristled brush to mix with, and a camel hair brush to apply the paint)

The American Woodcock

By Frank Russell

The woodcock project was presented as a 1998 seminar at my Stonegate Woodcarving School, and the photographs and carving sequences shown were taken as I taught.

The woodcock can be posed on a base in a strutting position, in a legs-down position, or without legs showing with chest and wing edges nestled on a base of leaves or forest litter. I often find them in this position when I wander through alder swamps and thickets. The position I used for this project also suggests a nesting bird.

As with any carving project, surround yourself with definitive and detailed references. You can't carve what you don't know. Generally, your carving is only as good as your best reference.

"I think the woodcock carving is great – But, I'm not sure I like the way it's mounted."

Materials & Tools

Materials:
- 4" x 5" x 9" tupelo
- Poster board
- Glue stick
- Hobby knife or scissors
- Glass eye (optional)
- Finishing materials of choice

Tools:
- Bandsaw or scroll saw
- 4 TPI skip-tooth blade

Carving Bits and Texturing Tools Schedule

Bit/Tool Number	Head Shape	Description	Head Size	Shaft Diameter
1 	Flame	Carbide bit	¾" W x 1" L	¼"
2 	Cylinder	Carbide bit	¾" W x ⅞" L	¼"
3 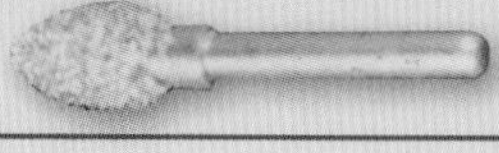	Flame	Carbide bit	⅜" W x ½" L	⅛"
4 	Flame	Carbide bit	¼" W x ⅜" L	3⁄32"
5 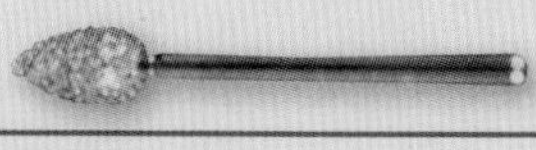	Flame	Ruby carver	¼" W x ⅜" L	3⁄32"
6 	Flame	Ruby carver	⅛" W x ¼" L	3⁄32"
7 	Ball	Ruby carver	⅛" Diameter	3⁄32"
8 	Tapered	Steel-fluted burr	⅛" W x ¼" L	3⁄32"
9 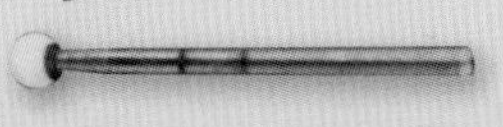	Ball	Aluminum/chrome oxide	⅛" Diameter	3⁄32"
10 	Cylinder	Aluminum/chrome oxide	3⁄32" W x ¼" L	3⁄32"
11 	Inverted Cone	Aluminum/chrome oxide	⅛" Dia.	3⁄32"
12 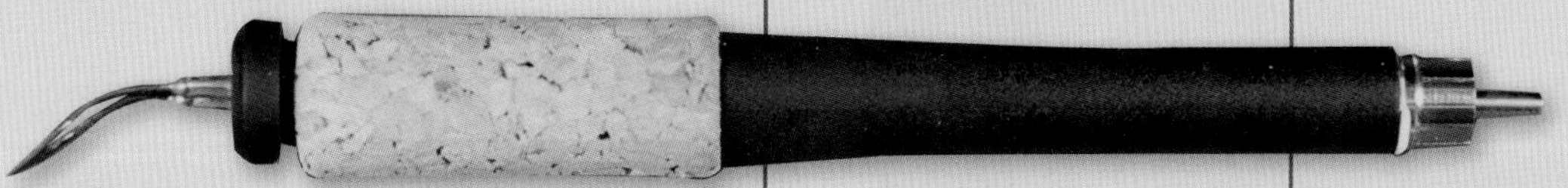	Bent Skew (dull edge)	Woodburner	5⁄16" W	N/A
13 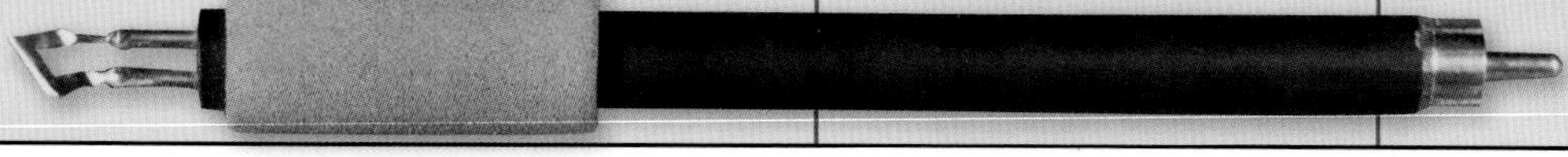	Skew (straight edge)	Woodburner	⅜" W	N/A

Preparing the blank

1 **Make patterns.** Using the working drawings, enlarge the side and top views and glue them to a piece of poster board with a glue stick. Cut the outlines out with a hobby knife or scissors. The woodcock can also be carved in a different scale: one-third, half, or quarter scale, for example.

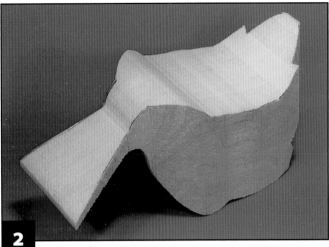

2 **Cut the block.** Start with a block of tupelo 4" wide by 5" high by 9" long. Use a ¼" 4 tpi (teeth per inch) skip-tooth blade to cut the side view first. Use the top and bottom waste pieces to cradle the blank. Tape the three pieces together with masking tape before cutting the top view.

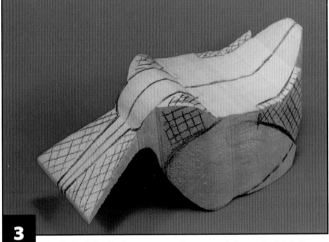

3 **Mark the blank.** Draw a centerline around the entire bird. Carve the bird with the head straight. Draw the top of the head, the beak, a shoulder line, and the upper line of the dropped wing. Use a broken line for the belly position. Leave plenty of stock for the wing curvature.

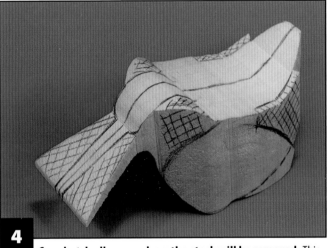

4 **Crosshatch all areas where the stock will be removed.** This is a safety reminder that allows you to more easily observe the symmetry of the entire bird. Crosshatching also reminds you to go back to areas that should be reshaped or don't look right.

5 **Using a flame-shaped carbide bit (1), remove all crosshatched areas.** Be sure to maintain symmetry from side to side. Carefully remove wood along both sides of the beak, and don't allow the bit to run around the front tip. Keep everything square at this point.

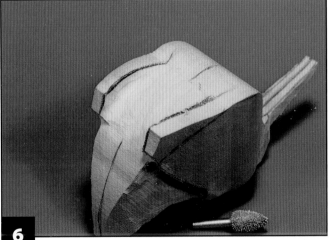

6 **Remove the waste wood between the legs.** Use the same flame-shaped bit to remove the crosshatched area between the legs on the underside of the bird.

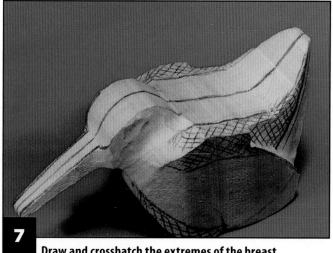

7 Draw and crosshatch the extremes of the breast, shoulders, and sides of the tail.

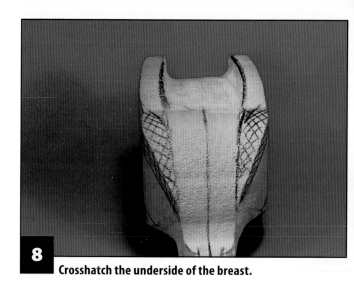

8 Crosshatch the underside of the breast.

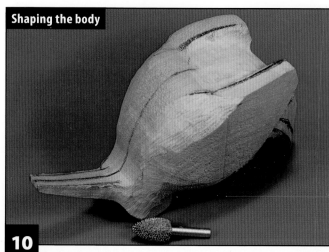

9 **Remove wood.** With bit #1 or #2, remove crosshatched areas, rounding toward the centerline.

Shaping the body

10 **Round the body.** As you round the body, think of the egg that this bird came from. Don't leave semi-rounded corners.

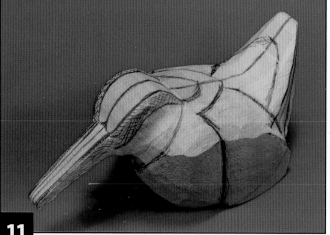

11 **Draw the head, bill, and major body areas.** Using a pencil, draw the extremes of the head and bill and crosshatch the areas to be removed. Draw shapes of major body contours and feather depressions such as the nape, cape, tail coverts, and wings.

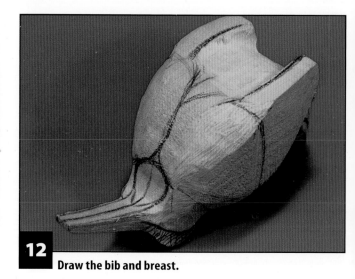

12 Draw the bib and breast.

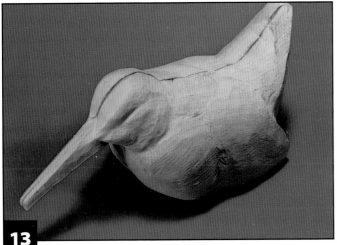

13 **Shape the major contours.** Use the small, flame-shaped carbide bit (#4) and a large, flame-shaped ruby carver (#5). Make the contours gracefully rounded and shaped to indicate which feather groups lie on top of one another.

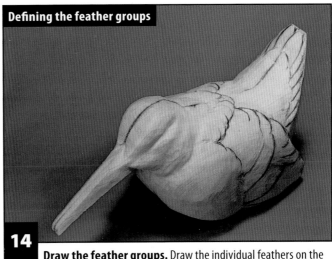

14 **Draw the feather groups.** Draw the individual feathers on the tail. Indicate the extremes of wing covert groups, tertials, and secondaries.

15 **Contour the areas in the previous step.** Use bits #4 and #5. Again, make all contours gracefully rounded and shaped to indicate which groups lie on top or under one another.

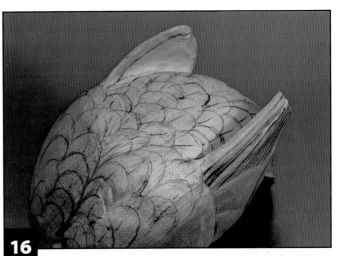

16 **Draw the body feathers on the underside of the bird.** This prepares for the rough shaping of the softer-appearing under feathers.

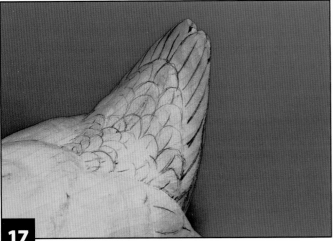

17 **Draw the tail feathers, tail coverts, and back feathers in preparation for rough shaping.** Also draw the hard wing feathers such as the primaries, secondaries, and tertials.

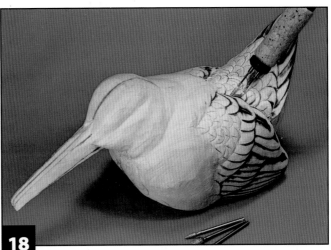

18 **Outline the feathers.** Do the tail feathers, tertials, lower wing coverts, secondaries, and primaries with the bent, skew-tipped woodburner (#12). Outline and shape the contour feathers (tail coverts, back, upper wing coverts, cape, and nape) with the large and small flame-shaped ruby carvers (#5 and #6). Finish shape and smooth with the tapered steel burr (#8).

Intermediate

19 Lay out the breast, flanks, and undertail coverts.

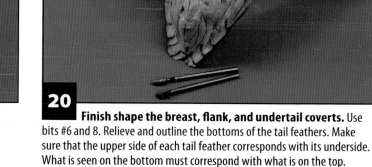

20 **Finish shape the breast, flank, and undertail coverts.** Use bits #6 and 8. Relieve and outline the bottoms of the tail feathers. Make sure that the upper side of each tail feather corresponds with its underside. What is seen on the bottom must correspond with what is on the top.

Carving the bill

21 **Rough shape the bill and draw the eyes.** Make the bill square. Then, draw the locations of eyes. At this time, draw the extremes of the jowl-ear area.

22 **Lay out the details of the bill.** Crosshatch the areas where you need the most control when removing wood. Also, lay out the underside of the bill.

23 **Finish shape and smooth all areas of the bill.** Use bits #6 and #8. Use 220-grit sandpaper to smooth the wood. Use the same bits to finish shape and smooth the underside of the bill.

24 **Cut in the bill separation and nostrils with the skew-tipped woodburner (#13).** Begin with a low heat setting until you establish the desired line. Then, increase the heat to deepen it. Cut in each eye cavity using the ball-shaped ruby carver (#7). Lay out and shape all head feathers.

25 **Set the eyes.** Use 10mm brown for a full-size woodcock. Be sure to texture the feathered areas around the eyes before placing. A texturing stone can ruin the glass. If the eyes are set before texturing is finished, cover the eye with a circular piece of electrician's tape.

26 **Lay out any remaining feather areas that were not done.**

27 **Final shape and smooth the feathers.** Do this over the entire bird in preparation for texturing.

Texturing

28 **Pre-texture all major feather groups with a ball-shaped bit (#9).** Keep the strokes in the same direction that you want the barbules of the feather to go. This makes the finish texturing much easier and gives the finished feather the little "bumps and rolls" that a real feather has.

Feather Texturing

I texture all working or stiff feathers with a woodburner. I find that burning in texture gives these feathers the same hard or stiff look that actual feathers have.

I texture all feathers that I consider contour or soft feathers with a cylinder-shaped or inverted cone texturing stone (#10 and #11). The stone gives these feathers a softer look than burning does.

I pre-texture all feathers, except the tiny ones on the head, with a ball-shaped stone (#9). The size of the feather determines the size of the ball shape I use. On a bird such as the woodcock, I can accomplish the entire pre-texturing operation with just one size.

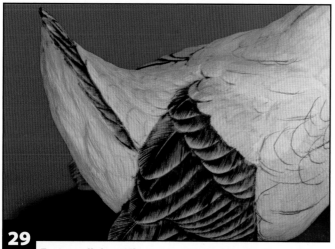

29 **Texture all the stiffer-appearing working feathers with the skewed-tipped woodburner (#13).** There may be areas where you are unable to get the feathered effect that you want with a wood burner. You can achieve a rougher looking feather edge by selectively texturing over the burn-textured edge with a cylinder-shaped or inverted cone texturing stone (#10 and #11).

30 **Finish texture the remaining bird with the cylinder-shaped or inverted cone texturing stone (#10 and #11).** Take the carving outdoors and check it under bright sunlight. More often than not, you will find one or more sections that could stand a bit of touchup with a texturing bit or wood burner. Then, the woodcock is ready for sealing, gessoing, and painting.

Legs and Feet

This project was designed to pose the finished bird in one of four positions:

1. Standing erect in a strutting pose with fully exposed legs and feet. This is a common position in the spring during mating season with the legs side by side or with the legs in a striding or walking position.

2. Standing in a crouched position with partially exposed legs and feet. The woodcock often stands in this position while listening for worm and grub movement underground.

3. Resting on the ground with no legs or feet showing. The toes may be partially exposed depending on depth of ground cover.

4. Nesting with body sunk deeply into ground cover. Showing toes is optional.

Unless well reinforced with wire, I do not think that commercially cast woodcock feet will support a bird of this size without bending or breaking. If carving for competition, I find most sponsoring organizations frown on cast feet anyway.

I prefer to make the feet and legs of a wildfowl myself. I can position my carving in any manner I want without fear of the legs breaking or the loss of the bird's natural appearance.

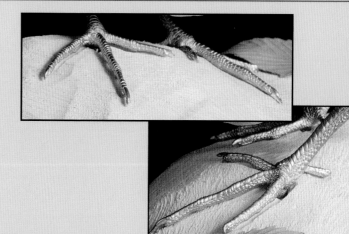

I do buy commercially cast bird feet for reference and sizing when I don't have a good natural specimen to work from. Along with the cast feet, I use photos of live specimens. Many consider using cast feet as a cheat, but used or not, they are invaluable as a reference. If the bird is not a competition bird, and it is in the resting position, I do use parts of the cast feet. I simply cut the toes off, sharpen the details with a jeweler's file if necessary, paint them, and use them under the bird.

No matter what the method of construction, realism is imperative so that the feet don't detract from the fine detail of the carving. When I am judging, I often see a good wildfowl carving that has poorly constructed feet. No matter what the quality of the carving, it doesn't place or, at best, it receives a lesser award.

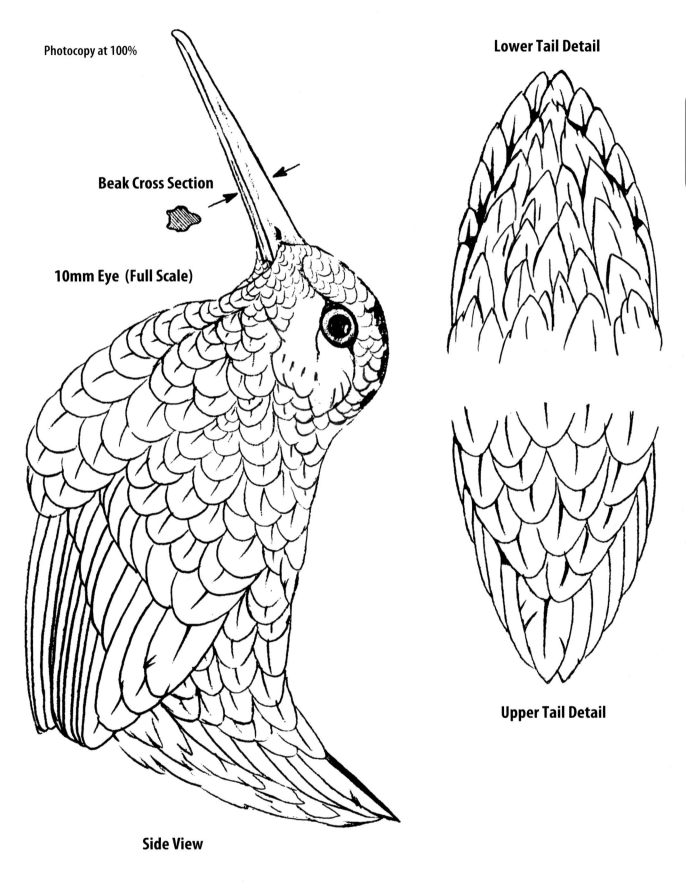

Photocopy at 100%

Lower Tail Detail

Beak Cross Section

10mm Eye (Full Scale)

Upper Tail Detail

Side View

Illustrations by Frank Russell

Underbill

Top View

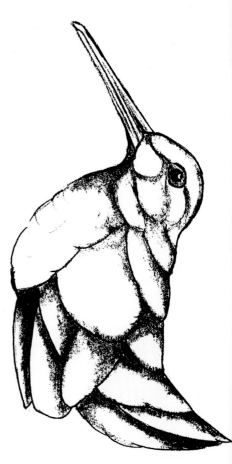

Feather Contours

Relief Carve a Whimsical House

By Jim Cline

I love to carve whimsical scenes in wood but hate the time it takes to prepare a relief carving for the detail stage using traditional methods. To solve this problem, I devised a way to block out the levels quickly using a rotary power carver equipped with a router attachment and spiral saw cutters to do most of the work. I discovered that if I use the cutters free-hand, I can create a unique texture that I have not been able to duplicate with any other tool.

Most of my carvings are made using construction-grade spruce and pine (2 x 12, 2 x 10, and 2 x 8 lumber). Because I'm not worried about messing up an expensive piece of wood, I experiment more and just carve away. I sell these pieces, which take me anywhere from 12 to 20 hours to carve, for up to $180. I can then turn around and spend that income on more wood and tools.

I prefer using power because the construction-grade lumber I use is hard to carve with hand tools. If you use basswood or something similar, you will get better results with hand tools. To carve in the different levels, I set my router attachment to the depth desired and block out the area with spiral saw cutters. Alternatively, you can use the spiral cutter to make a stop cut and clear the area out with a chisel.

NOTE: Spiral saw cutters are very aggressive. Using a Dremel with a router attachment instead of a router will help you gain some control. Practice this technique on a piece of scrap wood before beginning your carving.

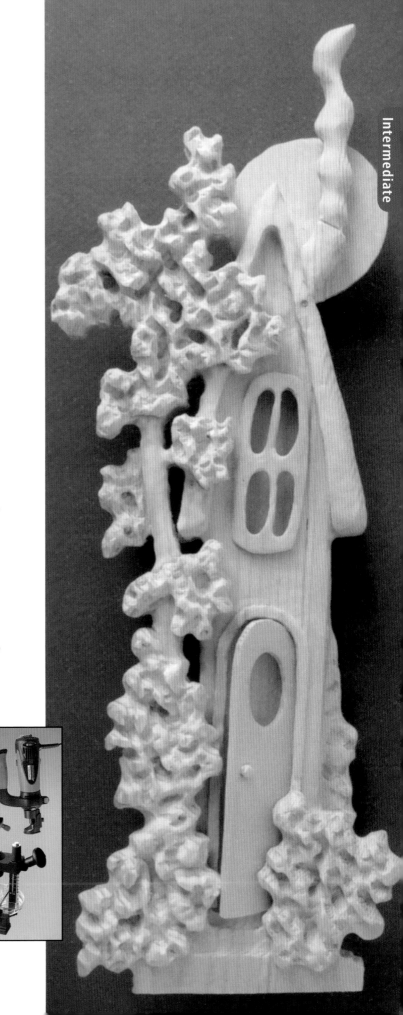

Here are high-speed rotary power carvers and a router attachment.

Roughing out

1 **Transfer the pattern to the work piece.** I slip a piece of carbon paper under the pattern and trace it onto the wood. Darken the perimeter of the pattern with a felt-tip marker to make it easier to rough out.

2 **Clamp the blank securely.** Attach a hardwood stick to the back of the blank to clamp it with. The stick also gets the carving up and off the bench. Screw the stick to the carving in the two places marked with an *x* on the pattern.

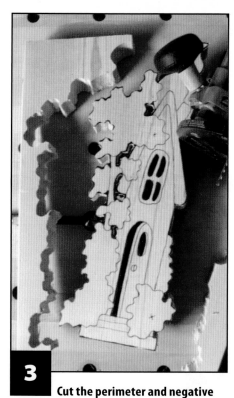

3 **Cut the perimeter and negative spaces.** I use a rotary saw tool. It takes a few passes to remove all of the waste wood. Don't forget the four small areas inside the outer perimeter. Clean up the sawdust with a shop vac.

4 **Rough out the back of the carving.** Temporarily remove the clamping stick from the back and attach it to the front. The area marked in black is to be removed. Take the area behind the smoke down ½". Remove ¾" of wood from behind the tree and the bottom left corner. Then, remove 1" of wood from behind the bush.

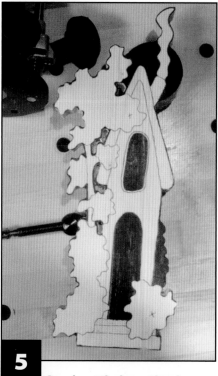

5 **Rough out the lowest levels on the front of the carving.** Reattach the hardwood stick to the back of the carving. Make several passes across the door, window, and moon. You want to carve away 1¼" of wood in the parts marked in black on the project.

6 **Carve down the walls of the house.** Use the spiral cutter to take ¾" off the areas marked in black on the project. Leave the area at the tip of the smoke there to support the base of the cutter and remove the tip with a chisel afterward.

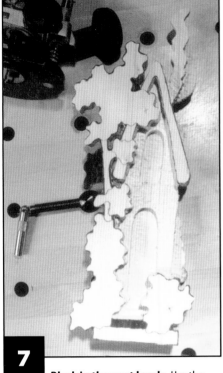

7 **Block in the next levels.** Use the spiral cutter to carve the doorstep and the rear tree leaves down $7/16$". I find it helpful to shade the entire section I am working on as a guide.

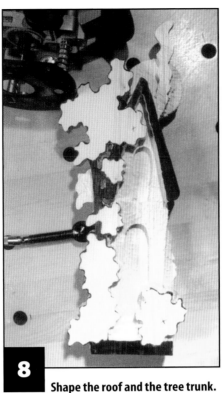

8 **Shape the roof and the tree trunk.** Take these areas down $5/16$" with the spiral cutter.

9 **Texture the leaves.** Use the spiral cutter free-hand in the rotary power carver to add short jagged lines for the leaves. Work from the outer edges in, and keep both hands on the tool.

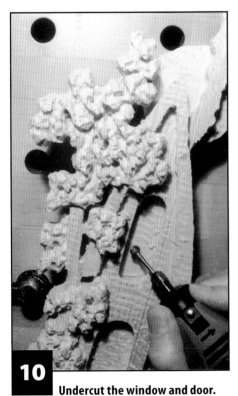

10 **Undercut the window and door.** The window is undercut on all four sides, but don't undercut the bottom of the door. Use a $1/4$"-diameter ball-shaped carbide bur. Leave the wood about $1/8$"-thick after undercutting.

11 **Undercut the tree and leaves.** Use a $1/2$"-diameter by $1/8$"-thick disc-shaped carbide bur. Use this same bur to undercut between the chimney and the smoke and between the tree and the moon.

12 **Shape the chimney and roof.** Round the front face of the chimney and smoke. Use a knife or chisel. Then, round the outer edge of the roof and a small amount of the tree trunk.

Intermediate

13 **Shape the moon.** Angle off the back side of the moon. Use a chisel.

14 **Make the door and window.** Trace the pattern for the window and door onto a piece of ⅛"-thick scrap. Make the window oversized so you can glue it over the frame. Carve out the panes with a cone-shaped carbide bur. Trim the door to fit, and glue it in place.

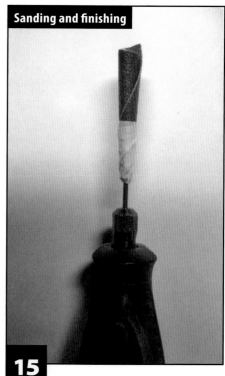

15 **Sand the carving.** Use a sanding mandrel loaded with Swiss sandpaper to remove any burrs and to smooth the surfaces. Start with 80 grit and use progressively finer grits up to 220 grit. Swiss sandpaper is more flexible and resists loading up when sanding the soft wood.

16 **Attach a hanger to the back of the carving.** Choose a place where the screws won't damage the front surface of the carving. Then, apply your finish of choice. I finish some of my carvings with a clear, satin, acrylic spray finish. If you use hardwood for your carving, boiled linseed oil mixed with turpentine is another option.

Materials & Tools

Materials
- 1½" x 8" x 12" pine or wood of choice
- 1" x 1" x 10" scrap of hardwood (To screw to the carving for clamping purposes)
- ⅛" x 1½" x 7" pine or wood of choice (window and door)
- Saw-tooth hanger
- Swiss sandpaper, assorted grits between 80 and 220 grit
- Finish of choice
- Carbon paper
- Wood glue

Tools
- Rotary power carver equipped with router attachment
- Assorted spiral saw cutters for the power carver
- Carbide burs: ¼"-diameter ball, small cone, and ½"-diameter by ⅛"-thick disc
- Sanding mandrel
- Chisel of choice
- Carving knife of choice

Carving Safety

The rotary tool used most in this type of carving is a ⅛" wood cutting bit. It can be used free-hand, but I suggest using it with an adjustable depth control or a router attachment.

If you do use it free-hand, the bit cuts very aggressively and may act like it has a mind of its own. It cuts best and is most controllable between 30,000 to 35,000 rpm. Just be cautious when using this tool. Keep the carving securely clamped down so you can use both hands on the tool. Replace the bit when it gets dull, and keep your body parts away from the moving bit.

Photocopy at 120% or desired size.

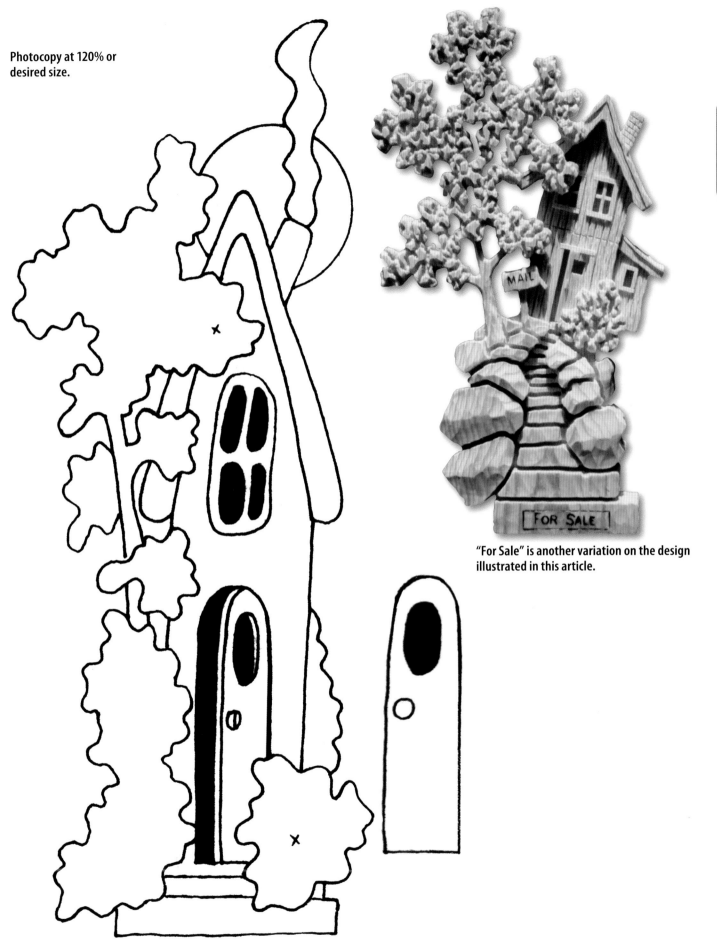

"For Sale" is another variation on the design illustrated in this article.

MAIL

FOR SALE

Intermediate

Decorative Cardinal

By Frank Russell

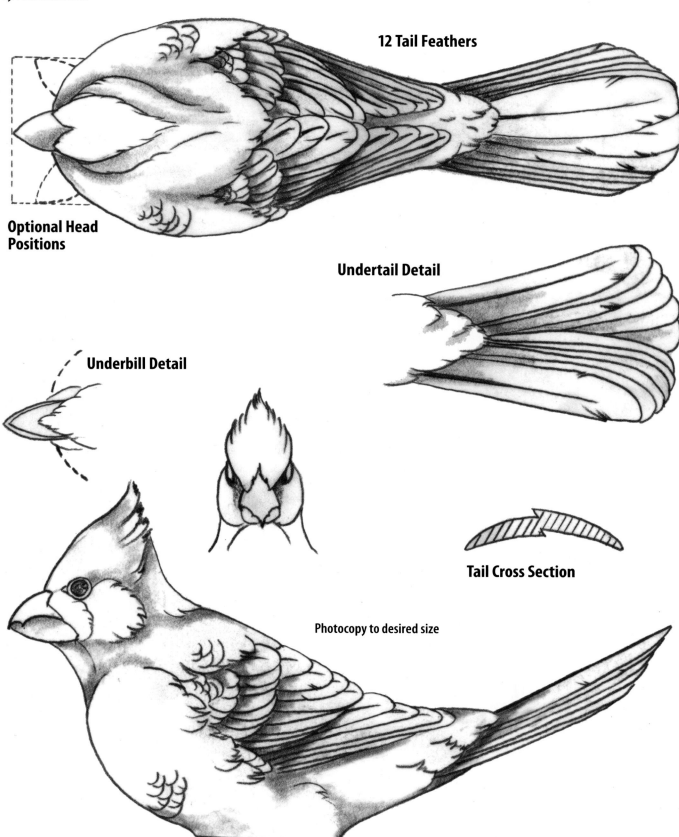

12 Tail Feathers

Optional Head Positions

Undertail Detail

Underbill Detail

Tail Cross Section

Photocopy to desired size

Now we come to the most ornery piece of wood that I have ever carved. I had a piece of Spanish Cedar that a vendor friend had given me at a woodcarving show. Just to check it, I smoothed one corner and textured a few feathers on it. They textured beautifully, so I blanked out the cardinal that follows.

All went well until I got to the texturing sequence, and the struggle began from there on. The wood had annular rings that were unbelievable—the wide rings textured nicely, but the narrow rings were as soft as balsa, and were filled with a resinous substance that clogged a texturing bit very quickly.

I was within a heartbeat of throwing it out and starting all over again, but New England tenacity made me continue. After completing the carving portion of the bird, the surface was such that I decided to paint it as a decorative carving as opposed to a realistic bird carving. I merely highlighted color areas and allowed much of the reddish wood to show through.

Materials & Tools

Materials:
- Wood of choice
- Glass eye (optional)
- Acrylic lacquer, varnish, or fine-grade, water-based sanding sealer
- Acrylic paints: cadmium orange medium, cadmium orange light, Mars black, raw umber, burnt sienna, burnt umber, cadmium red medium, cadmium red light

Tools:
- Band saw or scroll saw
- Small flame-shaped carbide bur
- Small and medium flame-shaped ruby carvers
- Small bud-shaped ruby carver
- Small inverted cone stone bit
- Small inverted cone diamond bit
- Rotary bristle brush

Advanced

Roughing out

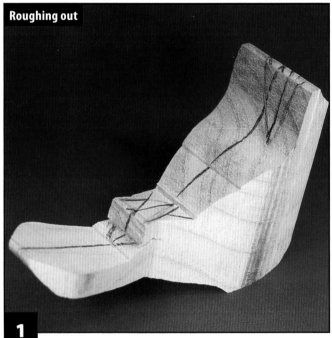

1 **Blank out the project on the bandsaw.** Draw a centerline all the way around the bird from tail to beak. Always honor your centerline. If you carve it away, draw it back in place again. Lay out the head and wings. Shape to these layout lines during the roughing out process.

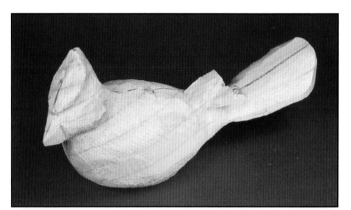

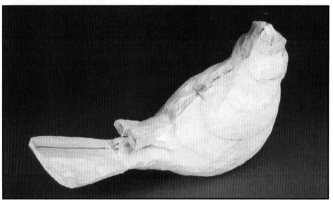

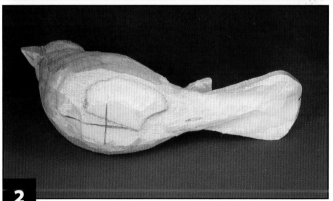

2 **Rough shape the bird.** Put in the head, body, wings, and tail. Use a small flame-shaped carbide bur and small and medium flame-shaped ruby carvers.

Defining feather groups

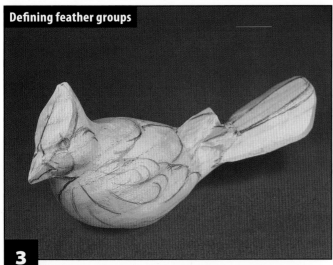

3 **Lay out the feather groups.** Make the cape, side feathers, cheeks, jowls, breast/bib indentations, and beak and eye location.

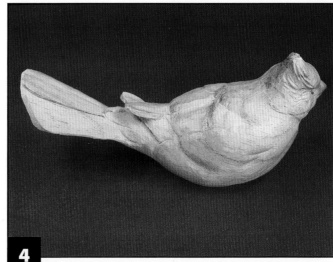

4 **Shape the feather groups.** Raise the cape away from the wing covert group, the coverts away from the wings, and one wing over the other. Separate the left side tail feathers from the right side by raising one away from the other. Use small and medium flame-shaped ruby carvers.

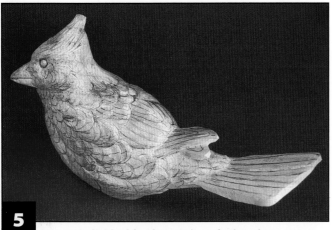

5 **Lay out individual feathers.** Indicate feathers that separate, overlaid feathers, and the direction of feathers. Draw lines to indicate the direction and turn the feathers will take. If these flow lines are pleasing to the eye, honor them as you texture by following in the same direction.

6 **Relieve feather separations, feather overlays, individual feathers, and feather accents.** On a real bird, some feathers break away from others, some lay over others, and some stand away by themselves. Carving these varieties into the feather pattern of your bird gives the carving a very pleasing effect. Don't overdo or you will have a bird that looks like as if it just flew through a turbine. Use small flame-shaped and small bud-shaped ruby carvers.

7 **Next, texture the feathers on the entire bird.** Texture from the rear forward and from the bottom upward. As you texture, occasionally allow a stroke to run down into the feather below if it is going in the same direction. This will give continuity and flow to the feather group. Use a small inverted cone stone bit, a small inverted cone diamond bit, and a rotary bristle brush for cleaning and defuzzing.

8 **Seal carving.** Use several thinned coats of acrylic lacquer or varnish or a fine-grade water-based sanding sealer. Allow the bird to dry thoroughly and then paint.

Painting Schedule

9 **Paint.** Paint the beak cadmium orange medium, highlighted with cadmium orange light. For the bib, use Mars black with raw umber. The irises are burnt sienna/burnt umber with Mars black/raw umber pupils. Paint the body feather highlights by dry brushing cadmium red medium with highlights of cadmium red light. Blend the outer feathers of the tail, wings, and wing coverts with a medium dark mixture of cadmium red medium and raw umber. Then, apply an antiquing wash to accentuate texturing highlights and major feather group indentations.

Black Bear

By Wanda Marsh

As an animal carver, I admit some of my best reference and inspiration comes from the Discovery Channel. I can not only view close-ups of the animals but also learn about their behaviors.

I saw enough videos and photographs of bears on rocks, especially ones preying on salmon, to know the pose I chose for this project would be enjoyed by other carvers. I kept the base and overall size compact because large pieces of wood, in this case basswood, are expensive, and when wood has to be laminated to obtain a big block, the cost is driven up considerably.

Power Carving

Whether I am working on animals or flowers, I rely on power carving tools. For roughing out the bear, I was able to remove wood very quickly with the aid of carbide cutters. To define some separation between the bear's paws and the rocks—the composition is carved from a single block of wood—I turned to fine diamond bits and ruby carvers.

For texturing the bear, I put several sizes of diamond discs to work. In less than three hours, I haired the entire animal. I also went over the texturing lines with a burning pen. The burn provides an extra tone, making the hair more realistic after paints are applied.

After roughing out, fine detailing, texturing, and burning, I still was not finished with the power tools. Because bits and burs tend to raise fuzzy grain in basswood, I cleaned up the bear with a rotary defuzzer.

Rocks are scarce in my area of Texas, so I purchased some from a garden center for reference. If you study a variety of rocks, you will find much more than meets the eye after a casual glance. Not only are there many textures, but there are also a variety of colors, especially earth tones, which happen to complement the bear. When carving the rocks, I took one extra step: I used hand tools to create and accentuate facets. If you sell power carved projects, you may have discovered some customers prefer a hand carved look and believe the piece is more valuable.

Painting Instructions

The process of painting the rocks tends to get messy, so start with them rather than the bear. Do not worry about minor problems such as an unpainted crevice. These can be corrected even after the bear is painted.

I prefer acrylic paints. They mix and blend well. Assemble the following colors, many of which are earth tones, and make a watery wash of each:

Burnt sienna
Burnt umber
Cadmium red
Charcoal black
Raw sienna
Raw umber
White

The secret to painting rocks is taking a "blotchy" approach while having the colors run together. Using the brush with a careless stroke, apply one color, then paint over it. Because there is no clear division of colors, neatness is not a priority. Do not bother to clean the brush as you change colors.

Some of the rocks should have more of one color than another. A very dark rock, for example, is base-colored in black with white applied sparingly. A brown rock is mostly raw umber with raw sienna highlights.

Photocopy to desired size

After applying at least two colors to each rock, spatter them with all of the colors listed above. To accomplish this, dip an old toothbrush into the washes. Pull a fingernail or the side of a pencil across the wet bristles to affect the spatter. Try out the painting process on scrap wood before tackling the project.

Before painting the bear, realize you do not want to cover the texturing and burn lines, which a heavy coat of paint will do. Instead, use several light washes of each color or mix.

Start with the muzzle by applying a mixture of white and raw sienna. Make sure this wash fades into the raw umber used for the rest of the body. To paint shadow areas—creases and the underside of the animal—add a small amount of black to the raw umber. To create a shadow around the nose and mouth, use a small amount of raw umber and black mixed together. Apply it with a dry brush.

For the eyes, take black straight from the tube, applying the paint in a nice even coat. Let it thoroughly dry. Next, mix raw umber and white to make a light brown tone for the irises. Let the paint dry. Paint the pupils black and let them completely dry. Paint a fine highlight or spot on the eyes using white from the tube. Finally, brush on a small line of cadmium red beside the pupils.

After the carving is completely dry, seal the carving with two to three coats of matte finish. Let each coat completely dry before spraying the next coat.

Mix together a small amount of five-minute epoxy, and with a toothpick, apply a dot to the center of each eye. Only a small amount is needed to cover the eyes. To keep the realistic look at its best, do not get any of the epoxy into the eye creases. When the adhesive is dry, carving fans will think that glass eyes were inserted.

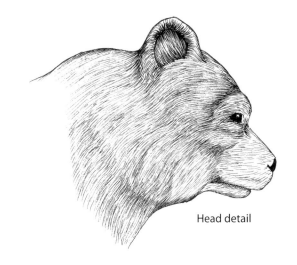

Head detail

Photocopy to desired size

Illustrations by Jack Kochan

Carving Realistic Habitats

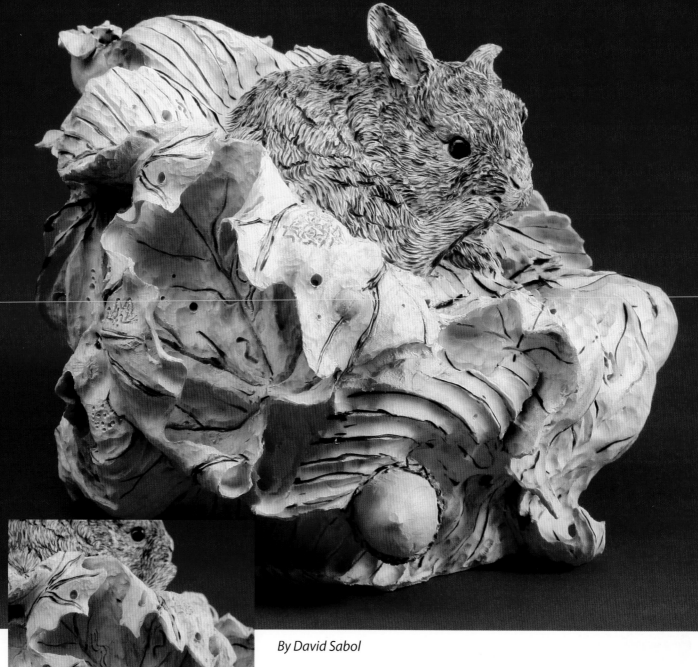

By David Sabol

I've always been fascinated with realistic wildlife scenes. I love combining different elements and adding hidden surprises that aren't always evident upon the first inspection. My new series of carvings—*Hidden in the Grass and Leaves*—plays with the way that a little critter's instincts to hide fight with its overwhelming curiosity.

Because of the realistic nature of these images, I found it was easier to power carve them out of one piece of tupelo. When carving the wood as thin as I need it for the realistic leaves, tupelo seems to be stronger than my customary white pine. The details of the leaves are just as important as the animal—realistic habitat can make or break your carving.

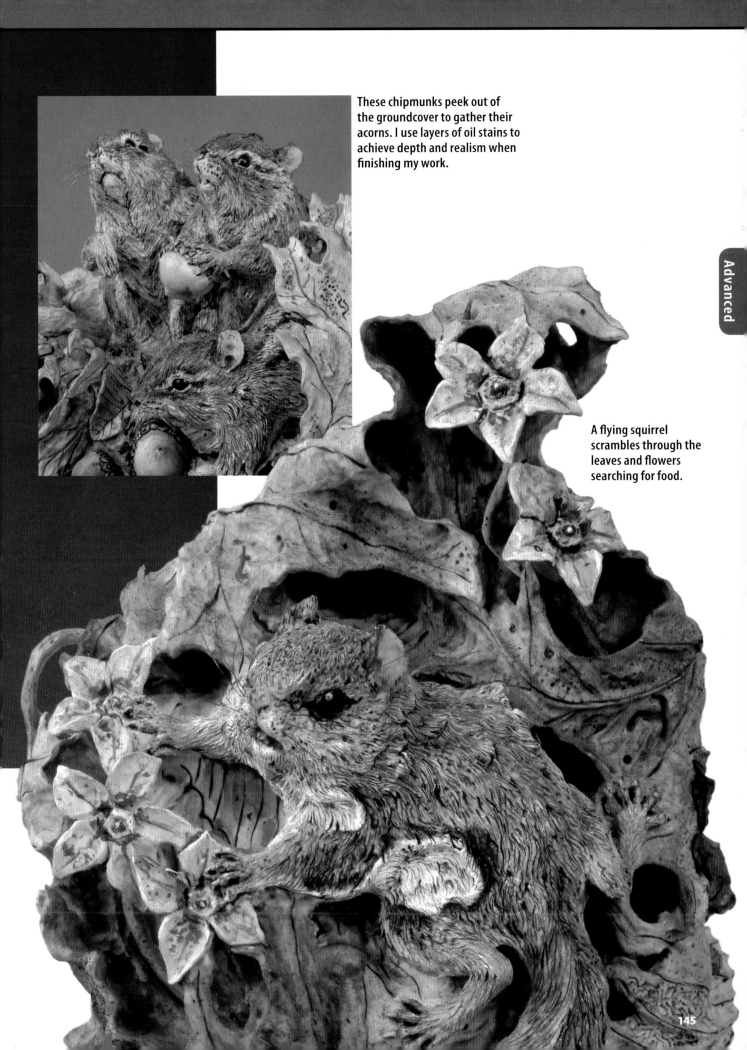

These chipmunks peek out of the groundcover to gather their acorns. I use layers of oil stains to achieve depth and realism when finishing my work.

A flying squirrel scrambles through the leaves and flowers searching for food.

1

Sketch the leaf onto the blank. I pick leaves that are curled up because they look more realistic and add texture to the carving. Keep the leaf handy to refer to while you are carving.

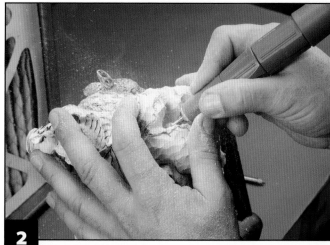

2

Hollow out the inside of the leaf. I alternate between a round and a half-round carbide bur. Don't be afraid to hollow out the inside deeply—this will let you give the leaf more curl.

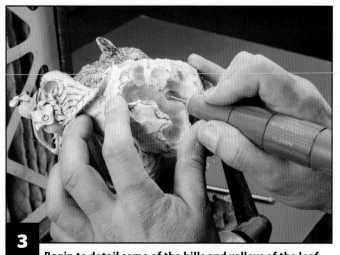

3

Begin to detail some of the hills and valleys of the leaf. Using the same burs, carve shallow ripples into the leaf. Refer to your real leaf often, and leave room for the veins, which will be detailed in later steps.

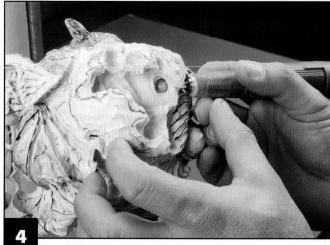

4

Hollow out the curls. After you finish roughing out the inside of the leaf, start detailing the curled part. At this point, leave the leaf thick, so you don't break it, but hollow it out so you can begin to see the general layout.

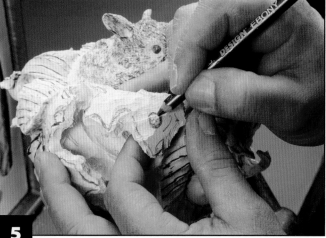

5

Pencil in the ladybug. My signature for this series is a ladybug in each carving. I decided to add one to this leaf now so I wouldn't forget. Sometimes I've had to go back and find a place to tuck one in. Outline the ladybug with a flame-shaped diamond bur.

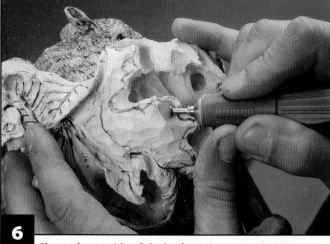

6

Shape the outside of the leaf. Use the same carbide burs you used to shape the inside of the leaf. Mirror the hills and valleys you carved on the inside of the leaf.

Thinning the leaves

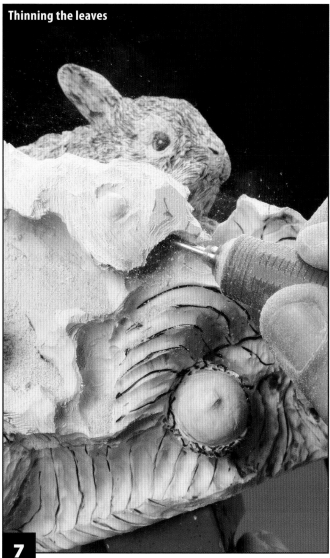

7 **Continue to thin down the main leaf and curled areas.** Work alternately on the outside and the inside to keep the shape of the leaf regular.

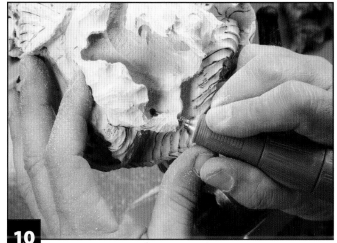

10 **Shape the smaller curls.** Switch to a small, round stump cutter. Be careful because the leaf is getting thin and fragile.

8 **Check the thickness of the leaf often.** Because the leaf is curled, you really can't use a measuring tool, but I've found that by pinching the wood between my thumb and index finger, I can gauge the thickness accurately enough.

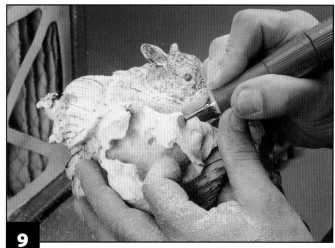

9 **Don't thin the leaf too much.** When I get close to my final thickness for the leaf, I keep one finger on the side opposite to the carving bur—that way I can tell exactly how thick the piece is while supporting the thin wood.

11 **Smooth off the inside of the leaf.** Switch to a flame-shaped ruby bur. Remove the marks left by the more aggressive burs and continue to refine the hills and valleys inside the leaf.

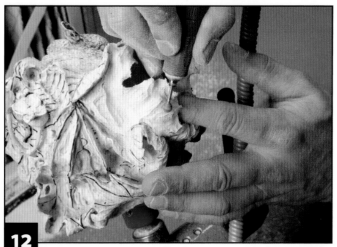

12 **Smooth the outside of the leaf.** Use the same ruby bur used to smooth the inside of the leaf.

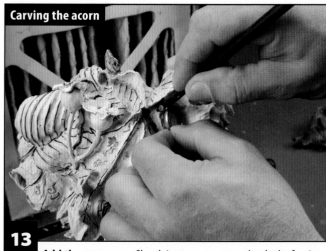

Carving the acorn

13 **Add the acorn cap.** Sketch in an acorn cap under the leaf, using a coin as a guide. Roughout the inside of the cap with a small round stump cutter. Switch to a round ruby bur before giving it a final shaping with a small round diamond bur. Smooth the inside with a white stone.

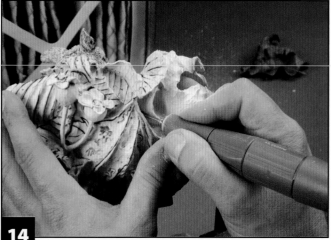

14 **Shape the outside of the acorn cap.** Switch to a thin, flame-shaped diamond bur. Round the outside of the acorn cap and undercut it so that it looks like it is stuck under the leaf.

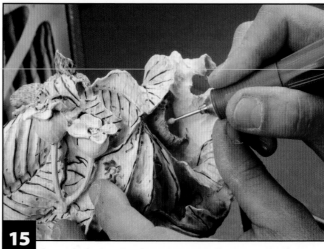

15 **Smooth the inside of the acorn cap.** Switch to a small, flame-shaped white stone. This will give you a very smooth finish. Be careful, because it is easy to clog and burn the stones. Dress the stone with a dressing stone or diamond hone to remove the clogged abrasive.

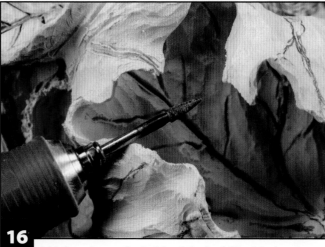

16 **Add the veins on the inside of the leaf.** Sketch in the veins, using your real leaf as a reference. Use the small, flame-shaped diamond bur to carve a line to simulate the recessed vein. Use the same bur to soften the transition between the main part of the leaf and the vein.

17 **Shape the vein on the outside.** Sketch the veins, using your leaf as reference. Use the diamond bur to carve a line on either side of the line you sketched. On the outside, you want a raised vein. Smooth the transition between the leaf and the vein and round over and shape the vein.

18 **Smooth the leaf.** I switch back and forth among a variety of different size flame-shaped white stones and round white stones. Get the leaf as smooth as possible now, before doing the final detailing.

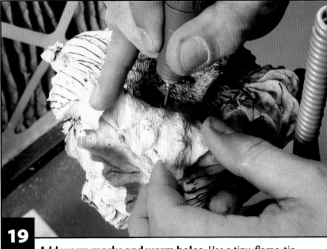

19 **Add worm marks and worm holes.** Use a tiny, flame-tip diamond bur to add fine lines and holes. You want the leaf to look like it has been on the ground for a while. Be careful, because it is easy to punch through the thin wood—too many worm holes makes the leaf fragile.

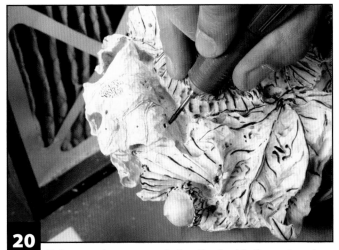

20 **Make some larger worm holes.** Use the thin, flame-shaped diamond bur to make roughly-circular holes that are surprisingly realistic.

Materials & Tools

Materials
- Tupelo of choice (depending on the project)
- Curled leaf of choice (I used a maple leaf)

Tools
- Flexible shaft tool or micro motor of choice
- Small round carbide bur
- Small half-round carbide bur
- Small round stump-cutter
- Small round ruby bur
- Flame-shaped ruby bur
- Thin flame-shaped diamond bur
- Flame-shaped diamond bur

- Small round diamond bur
- Tiny flame-tip diamond bur
- Small flame-shaped white stone
- Very small flame-shaped white stone
- Small round white stone
- Very small round white stone
- Dressing stone or diamond hone
- Woodburner with pen of choice
- Pencil
- Nickel
- Gesso
- Flow medium
- Acrylic paints

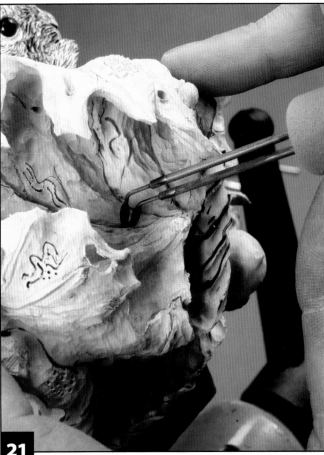

21 **Highlight the veins.** Use a woodburner. I commissioned Optima to make a custom long, bent woodburning tip specifically so I could get into the deeply curled leaves. They call it the David Sabol extended 45°-angle tip, but use whatever tip works best for you. Line the large veins and draw the thinner veins free-hand with the woodburner.

Index

Contributors

Jim Cline

Jim Cline took up woodcarving when he retired in 1987, has taken home a number of ribbons, and has taught woodcarving at the Naramata Center in Canada.

Lori Corbett

Lori Corbett has been carving since 1986 and offers classes in bird carving at her studio in St. Anthony, Idaho, where she resides with her husband. www.whisperingeagle.com.

Lynn Diel

A carver who enjoys designing his own very affordable carving tools and accessories, Lynn Diel was the winner of *WCI's* first Poor Man's Tool Contest held in 1998.

Jack Kochan

Jack Kochan has been a frequent contributor to and illustrator for *Woodcarving Illustrated* and makes his home in Leesport, Pennsylvania.

Wanda Marsh

Wanda Marsh is a professional carver, author, and instructor who lives with her husband in New Caney, Texas.

Frank Russell

Frank is an 11th generation Vermonter from a long line of diverse artisans and craftsmen. He has won many carving competitions both in the United States and Canada, and has judged at numerous shows, including the Ward Foundation World Competition in Ocean City, MD.

David Sabol

David Sabol is a professional woodcarver and instructor and a member of the Caricature Carvers of America. www.davidsabol.com

Chuck Solomon and Dave Hamilton

Chuck Solomon and Dave Hamilton are avid carvers and instructors and have co-authored several books together.

Kenny Vermillion

Kenny Vermillion has been carving wildlife subjects professionally since 1983. His works have won hundreds of awards and are in private and museum collections throughout the U.S. and seven other countries. www.kennyvermillion.com

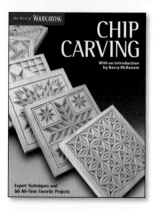
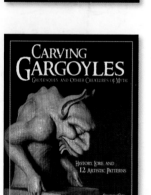
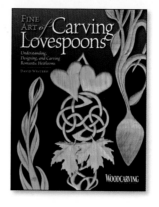
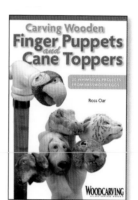